Runway

to

Recoveries

45 YEARS: FROM AIRPORT PLACES
TO CHILDREN'S FACES

To Kelly,

For all of those whom she put on the recovery path!

JEFF DEGNER

Jeff Degner 2020

Wasteland Press
www.wastelandpress.net
Shelbyville, KY USA

Runway to Recoveries:
45 Years: From Airport Places to Children's Faces
by Jeff Degner

First Printing – October 2021
ISBN: 978-1-68111-441-5

Printed in the U.S.A.

0   1   2   3   4   5

PREFACE

As a customer service agent for Delta Air Lines at Chicago's O'Hare International Airport, primarily in the departure gates, my career spanned more than four decades. During this time, I experienced an amazing number of unique, funny, stressful, dangerous and truly unexpected passenger-related incidents. For years, my family and friends begged me to put them all down in writing. *Runway to Recoveries* is the *second* result of that endeavor, the first being *What Track for the Atlanta Flight* published last year. *Runway to Recoveries* is a dual presentation. The first part continues *What Track for the Atlanta Flight* with many untold stories, plus a few bits of airport trivia you might find interesting. I'm hopeful that these new tales will make you smile or sigh, just as I did when I recalled them all. Whether involving passengers or fellow employees, I've been blessed with a multitude of vivid recollections.

The stories are as I remember them - except that in most cases the names have been changed to protect the innocent!

These challenging or memorable situations all occurred over a period where I established and polished the traits of "Jeff Degner, Delta Gate Agent" that so many people still recall, though I've now been retired since 2015. Likewise, these same traits also helped me to gladly move along a path, a "runway" if you will, which led to my involvement with the non-profit charity called Healing the Children. I've now been associated with Healing the Children (HTC) for more than 30 years. The latter part of this book will relate some of the incredible recovery stories I've been fortunate enough to experience. The title, therefore, is most appropriately called, *Runway to Recoveries.*

Among its goals, Healing the Children strives to bring vital health aid to children with medical needs who would otherwise never receive care. These underprivileged young people can be from around the world or around the block.

Part of the HTC mission involves bringing kids here to the USA, using qualified escorts, for vital surgeries not available in their own countries. Once here, they stay with appropriate and vetted host families.

Equally important for HTC activities is creating medical missions to Third World countries where a team of professionals sees or treats many sick or injured children in a local hospital. It has been my joy to have escorted dozens of kids to or from such places as Nicaragua, Honduras and El Salvador. I've also organized and then participated in eleven medical missions, both as a photographer and translator.

I've regularly seen the love our American host families have poured out to the children who have stayed with them for weeks or months, treating them just like their own sons or daughters.

Because of my Delta connections, I've arranged for flight attendants and pilots to act as escorts which they have done with enthusiasm. Most report that their trips were life-changing events, for them as well as for the kids. They beg me to ask them again!

Other airline friends have become host families, and some have accompanied HTC medical teams as translators. The all have their own stories to share – stories about young lives that they helped change. Every HTC volunteer: doctors, nurses, escorts, host families, joyfully gives of their time and expertise – and they are ever willing to give some more.

Finally, the images that fill me with the most happiness are the before-and-after scenes that I've been able to glimpse, long after a once-suffering child has become a healthy, happy adult.

So, dear readers, as you peruse the two parts of this little book, I hope part one makes you laugh, squirm and sigh. Then, I hope part two makes you both grateful and appreciative for what you have. Know that I feel just like every other Healing the Children volunteer I've ever met: **lucky**! Lucky to be able to help others a little…lucky to feel such tremendous joy in doing so…lucky to be able to get others involved with HTC…and now, lucky to be able to share all of these unique adventures with you.

Fasten your seat belts!

PART ONE
Airport Stories

AIR FRIGHT EXPERIENCES

Before working at the Delta terminal, I spent about a year in the Air Freight department. Our cargo facility was just outside of the main runways and taxiways at O'Hare. There were two incidents which occurred during my single year there, and I'll never forget either.

Fork it Over

It was a wet, dark and windy night as thunderstorms overtook the O'Hare area. Despite the weather, one of our large cargo forklifts had to be driven from the other side of the airport, where our maintenance facility was, back to the cargo area. I knew the routes to take and volunteered to make the drive. I got a ride to the maintenance building in a ramp tug, splashing through puddles all the way. There, I garbed myself completely in rain gear, including a hood, and soon I was off, driving the big forklift (it was probably ten feet high) scooting along the access roads and stopping at the occasional taxiway to let a plane go by. Initially, it was kind of fun, at least for a while. The rain was warm, and the lightning made the entire airport area look spooky and unreal. Of course, I also (too late) realized how vulnerable that big forklift was for a bolt of lightning! Nevertheless, there I was, merrily on my way, our cargo facility ever nearer, when I turned off the access road and onto the final roadway which would take me directly there.

I was terribly wrong. Temporarily blinded by the rain, or perhaps dazzled by the lightning, I had turned too soon. Within moments, I realized I was not on the appropriate roadway, but instead, on an *active taxiway*. Dear God!

Fortunately, I knew another access road would intersect the taxiway in the distance, and I felt relieved.

But then I heard a roaring sound behind me and saw an ENORMOUS PLANE taxiing right in my direction. Can you imagine my terror? I floored the gas on the forklift, pulled to the left as far as I could possibly go and, looking behind me, still saw the plane inexorably getting closer. AND CLOSER. And then *its wing passed directly over the top of the forklift*. Not even a bump! No sweat! Except for the sweat pouring off me, mingled with the warm rain. The pounding of my heart seemed even louder than the thunder at that point.

Even as I write these words, some 50 years later, my heartbeat still races in recalling my horror of that stormy night. I can only imagine the radio call the plane may have made to the O'Hare control tower:

"Tower, this is United 201 on taxiway 22R. We've just passed over someone driving a big forklift down our taxiway in the pouring rain! You might want to check it out"

"Tower to United, can you please repeat? And can you describe the driver or the airline he is associated with?"

"Tower, the man was covered in rain gear, and we could see no airline identification on him or the forklift. We only got a view of his face as we passed by. He was as white as a sheet"

Tumbling Act

Occasionally, we'd be visited and inspected by Delta's Chicago Station Manager, Gene. His office was located just below our airport concourse and, thus, he'd need to be driven across O'Hare property to get to the Air Freight building. Often, he was accompanied by other management people. One day, after his inspection and meeting with Mac, our cargo manager, Gene needed a ride back to the Delta concourse. Also with him would be Lou, who was the overall manager of customer service for Delta. Incidentally, Lou was one responsible for approving promotions for cargo employees seeking to get into public contact, like me.

When the time came to drive Gene and Lou back to the airport, Mac decided to come along for the ride. However, the Delta station wagon normally used for this type of transportation was not available. Instead, the only vehicle that could be used was the cargo van.

"Can anyone drive a stick shift?" came the call.

"Sure!" I said.

Therefore, I soon found myself in the driver's seat of the cargo van. Unfortunately, there was only one other seat, the passenger seat. The rest of the van was totally empty. So, Gene, by virtue of his title as Station Manager, sat in the single passenger seat. Lou and Mac simply held on to the back of the two front seats, directly behind us.

I hadn't driven a stick shift in several years, but I was very confident in what I was about to do. However, as I tried to smoothly shift into first gear, I ACCIDENTALLY POPPED THE CLUTCH! The van suddenly lurched forward, and I could plainly hear "ARRRGGGHHH! (as well as other unpleasant words) as both Mac and Lou lost their grips on the front seats and tumbled behind. OMG! Right then and there I feared my job was over, or at least my chances for promotion. Somehow, though, the two men picked themselves up, resumed their now-nervous positions standing behind the seats, and we started off again. This time I delivered them safely to the airport. My clutch work came through in the clutch! A few weeks later I was promoted to public contact and the rest is history.

WALLED UP

Before 9-11, anyone could enter the airport concourses at almost any time as there were no security checkpoints. Consequently, dozens of homeless people would ride the subway from Chicago to O'Hare, spending the night there, warm and safe, sleeping on the concourse floors or in gatehouse chairs, even though airline employees and O'Hare police constantly asked them to move. Most folks don't realize this, but the visible walls of the gatehouses are not very massive at all. In fact, they are more like sturdy partitions. They look nice and do a good job of separating one gate from another. However, hidden (and protected) behind them are the actual concrete and steel beams that make up the airport's superstructure. These false walls include one special panel which actually is a cleverly disguised door. It opens by way of a keyhole at the bottom. Occasionally, an airport facility worker leaves one of the wall doors unlocked. It was a rumor among us that there was at least one time when a vagrant found such an unlocked door and immediately claimed the space inside as his personal residence, coming out only at night and at times stealing food from airport vendors.

One early morning, I was the first to arrive at my assigned gate. As I stepped behind the desk and started assembling paperwork, I happened to look over towards the wall. The door to the inner cavity was open slightly. Holy cow! So, I took the opportunity to quietly and, I admit, nervously, open that secret door a bit wider to look inside. The area it revealed was dark and surprisingly big, extending all the way to the back of the gatehouse. Once my eyes got accustomed to the dimness, I ventured inside, deeper and deeper. In the distance, I could see a chair with an airline blanket draped over it. With that discovery, I realized the rumor was true. Somebody had spent a lot of time in that hidden space. Wow!

As I made my way back to the hidden door, I realized that it had closed behind me somewhat and was now only slightly ajar. Yet, as I reached to push it open, I distinctly heard the voice of one of my colleagues on the other side, talking to another agent.

"Hey! There's a door here! And it's open! I wonder where it leads to?!"

Instantly I stepped back and quietly melted into the darkness.

"I'm going to see what's inside!" the voice said, sounding excited yet leery.

Slowly...cautiously...the door opened, and my colleague stepped into the darkness.

That's when I grabbed him and yelled, "Arggghhhhhhhh!"

I've never heard a man scream so loud. The terrified words he used at the top of his lungs, echoed up and down the entire concourse. Then, he leaped back into the gatehouse as fast as humanly possible, getting away from whoever or *whatever* was inside the wall. I can't imagine what the passengers sitting nearby must have thought.

Those false walls and hidden doors still exist in the gate areas of O'Hare. Check it out the next time you're there. But whatever you do….DO NOT GO INSIDE!

A LITTLE MISTAKE

A Delta PSA (Passenger Service Agent) is entrusted with more responsibility than a regular agent. Besides having a warm, outgoing personality, he or she is supposed to be able to make quick decisions, soothe angry customers and be quite capable with problem-resolution. Throughout my years at Delta, my most favorite job of all was Gate PSA, and most of the stories in this book came about because of actions I took in that position. During my initial weeks of being a gate PSA, I was still getting used to just how much responsibility I had. This came to a memorable head one day when I got a frantic call from the ticket counter, stating that a family of five had been detained at check-in and were now rushing to the gate for their flight which was leaving in just 15 minutes. At that time there was no TSA check point. So, I decided to wait for them, even if it meant delaying the flight a minute or two.

They all got to the gate just at departure time and were so delighted that we'd waited for them, realizing that we'd gone above and beyond to do so. However, by the time they were seated on board and the plane pushed back, it was two minutes late.

"No big deal," I thought, recalling those five last-minute happy passengers. However, that's when my supervisor, Frank, learned about that "little" delay. Yikes! He said, "MEET ME IN MY OFFICE, DEGNER!" and, in doing so, found myself the victim of the worst tongue-lashing I've ever received. He was *furious* that he hadn't first been consulted about my decision. He was more furious that we'd taken a delay. He YELLED at me! So, I YELLED back, trying to justify my actions. Other agents walking down the hall could hear our outbursts and were probably worried about the future of my job.

Eventually, Frank and I had a more respectful dialogue about what had happened, and I learned something new, besides the fact that I should have let him know.

When airlines *share* a taxiway, as Delta did at that time, both airline's gate departures are carefully choreographed by the O'Hare control tower, with each plane's back-out time ensuring that the taxiway is constantly, smoothly, in use. If a plane is late, however, even two minutes, that choreography is messed up! Therefore, rather than being first in a line of departing flights, that same plane could end up being last. Worse, that little two-minute delay could morph into a thirty-minute delay by the time the plane takes off, resulting in passengers missing their connections. Therefore, this is why airplanes now always back out early – sometimes VERY early – rather than miss their chance in the lineup on the taxiway.

I didn't know this back then. But, Frank sure did and after our discussion became more normal, I sincerely apologized and never made those mistakes again.

Unhappily, there was more to come. Frank's boss, a man whose title was "Coordinator" wanted to yell at me too. Sadly, he also had the bad habit of spewing spittle when he was really mad. Which he was. "DEGNER", he shouted, "I'M THE COORDINATOR AND EVEN I CAN'T MAKE THAT DECISION! WHAT IN GOD'S NAME WERE YOU THINKING? YOU DIDN'T BOTHER TO TELL FRANK, EITHER!" All I could do was apologize – quietly. Truth be known, I did learn several valuable lessons that day, though I wish I could have learned them without such drama and spittle!

BAKED GOODS

Throughout my Delta gate agent career, I frequently worked busy flights with dozens and dozens of anxious standby passengers, many of whom were "non-revs" or fellow airline employees. Often, I would make this announcement: "For those of you who are on standby, if you have any home-baked pastries, this will increase your odds of getting on the flight." Even though this clearly wasn't true, the announcement invariably brought smiles to everyone in the gate house, including those not standing by! I also received countless gifts of cookies, donuts, and even healthy granola bars which I *sometimes* shared with my fellow employees.

One day, I noticed a teenaged young man slowly but deliberately approaching my gatehouse. It was clear that he suffered from a physical impairment and I suspected it was cerebral palsy. As he made his way towards me, his arms and legs were crooked and ungainly, yet still carried him straight to where he now stood directly in front of me.

"Can I help you?" I asked.

He slowly and haltingly replied, "I. Brought. You. Some. Home. Baked. Pastries. Jeff." Then he beamed and brought out from behind his back a tantalizing package of brownies.

I was almost speechless. I also recognized him as Adam, the son of a Delta employee at O'Hare.

"Thank you so much, Adam," I said. "What a wonderful surprise!" In the distance I spied his mom, smiling at our conversation. I knew she had made those brownies.

I spontaneously stepped out from behind the podium and held out my arms for a hug of gratitude. Without hesitation, Adam stepped into my gentle embrace.

It was somewhat more difficult for him to get his own arms into position. But it was one of the nicest hugs I have ever had. Ever after, we always greeted each other with the same kind of enthusiastic, warm embrace. The last time I saw him, he was heading to Honolulu where he was enrolled in the University of Hawaii. Somehow, I know that Adam is now living a bright future.

O'HARE TRIVIA PAGE 1

When was the first landing in the area now known as O'Hare? The answer is...MILLIONS of years ago. If you Google "Des Plaines Disturbance," you will find articles that aren't referring to civil unrest, but rather to the impact of a large meteor that left a five-mile-wide crater encompassing part of what is now O'Hare. The amount of energy released by this impact was comparable to several thousand hydrogen bombs! The crater itself became filled in after the last Ice Age. However, to this day, about 100 feet below the surface, there is a thick layer of compacted rock. That layer was caused by the first landing at O'Hare.

****

During the construction of Runway 27L, excavators uncovered the remains of native Americans. Such Indian burial grounds are common in the area. For hundreds of years, the nearby Des Plaines River was used by various original tribes, including Pottawatomi, Fox and Sauk. In fact, "Black Hawk" was an infamous chief of the Sauk, from whom the Chicago hockey team got its name. The Indian bones uncovered were disinterred and re-buried in a mass grave, located in a tiny cemetery just off the airport property, on Irving Park Road. However, <u>not all</u> those old bones could have been recovered. Thus, every airplane landing on 27L today is undoubtedly coming down on what's left of an ancient Native American gravesite. Think about that as you prepare for landing!

ACHOOO

A new gate agent, named Jerry, began working with me at O'Hare. I became his on-the-job training instructor, and soon we were friends. We also were VERY competitive with each other, ranging from who was the better racquetball player to who was faster in processing the details of a busy flight. One day, while working together, my back happened to be turned when, suddenly, I heard a very short but faint sound coming from Jerry. It sounded like "choooop!"

"What was that sound?" I asked.

Jerry replied, "It was me. I sneezed."

"Huh? I hardly heard anything!"

"I know" he said, "I've taught myself to hold it in"

I was incredulous. A few weeks later the same thing happened, this time in front of my disbelieving eyes.

"Choooop!"

I had witnessed another of Jerry's quiet sneezes. He simply shrugged, like it was no big deal at all.

After this second episode, my competitive spirit leaped into action, and I was determined to teach myself how to hold a sneeze in, *even better* than Jerry could. Therefore, later in the day and back at home, I felt that familiar tickle in my nose. I knew my sneeze was imminent, so I decided to attempt his quiet technique.

HUGE MISTAKE!! My eyeballs practically jettisoned from their sockets. My nasal passageway sent a huge volume of air towards my brain, and I thought my skull was going to explode. I saw stars, had an instant headache and my heart went into unusual palpitations.

I never tried it again for fear of death. Jerry went on to transfer departments and became a Delta flight attendant. To this day, he doesn't know about my near catastrophe.

FACING THE REDS

One of my favorite high school teachers was my Spanish teacher, Mr. Vince Giamalva. He was a great instructor, personable and knowledgeable, and made learning Spanish, fun. One of the things I remember most about him, though, was how he vividly blushed whenever he felt uncomfortable. His face just seemed to turn bright red with the slightest embarrassment, and we students loved eliciting that reaction.

One day I discovered that Vince and his wife, Kathy, both retired from teaching, were booked on the Delta flight I was working. Hmmm! Soon enough I could see them in the distance, walking towards my gate.

I accessed the O'Hare paging system and announced, "Vince Giamalva, return to the Delta ticket counter"

Mr. Giamalva stopped., looked around, glanced at Kathy questioningly, then shook his head as if he'd heard the announcement wrong. They both then continued towards my gate.

Again, I accessed the airport public-address system and this time, in a louder, more authoritative voice said, "VINCE GIAMALVA, RETURN TO THE DELTA TICKET COUNTER IMMEDIATELY"

By now, Vince and Kathy had almost reached the gate, not realizing that I was the agent there. Slowly, Mr. Giamalva handed his carry-on baggage to Kathy and started back towards the ticket counter area, looking worried.

This is when I caught up with him and gently tapped him on the shoulder.

He turned around, saw my big grin, and broke into the reddest blush ever! Then, he said, threateningly, "You know, Jeff, as a former teacher, I can still go back into your high school records and change your Spanish grade to an F." Ha!

Vince, Kathy and I had a brief reunion, but then it was time for me to return to my gate and continue working the flight they were on. But I wasn't done with them yet.

At departure time, I went onto their plane and made one more announcement. Vince and Kathy were probably in their early 50's at the time. I knew exactly where they were seated. This is what I said:

"Ladies and gentlemen, just wanted you to know that the couple in Seats 20A and B are celebrating their 75th wedding anniversary! "

A scattering of congratulatory applause ensued and as I looked back into the area of the plane where the Giamalvas were sitting, I could clearly see a glow of red emanating from *both* of their faces. *Olé!*

GASP!

All the arriving passengers had deplaned off the Delta flight I was meeting, or so I thought. A single flight attendant. Kathy, was next, but she stopped and said, "Jeff, there's someone on board who appears to be sleeping. We can't wake her up."

I followed Kathy back onto the plane and sure enough, occupying a middle seat near the back of the plane was a woman who seemed to be sound asleep.

Quietly, I said to the woman, "Ma'am? Ma'am? Hello? Hello?"

No response.

I tried again, a little louder, while gently touching her shoulder, "Ma'am? Hello? Time to wake up!"

Still no reply. In fact, she started to snore.

I suppose I could have jostled her more firmly, but I hesitated to do so, because this is when I knew I had the chance to try something I'd always wanted to do.

At the time of this incident, all Delta planes were equipped with ammonia capsules – something akin to smelling salts – that, when broken apart, allowed ammonia to be released, causing a sleeping soul to gently awaken if other methods had failed.

"Get me the ammonia inhalants!" I said.

Within moments I had in my hand a little orange capsule. Looking back at the situation now, I realize that I should have held it away from our dozing passenger's face.

But then, as Kathy and her crew all watched with bated breath, I held the capsule directly under her nose and cleanly broke it in half. The results were almost instantaneous. In one brief second, her nostrils flared. One second later, she gasped – and loudly, too! Then, just one millisecond after that, she was completely awake, eyes bulging and arms quivering, as she jerked, bolt-upright in her seat. Wow.

"Good morning!" I said, "Welcome to Chicago!"

I helped her gather her belongings and happily escorted her off the flight. Years later, such inhalants were banned from commercial flights, as the strong, immediate reactions they caused also led to far more dangerous situations, like heart attacks or strokes. Whew!

SPEAK NOT

One day a young man approached me at my gatehouse desk and said that he had something important to tell me. First, he gestured to two other passengers, both men and both dressed in saffron-colored, flowing robes. They were high-ranking members of an Eastern religion, he said, traveling on Delta for a world-wide conference. The young man described himself as a "devotee" and "personal assistant" and that his job was to help them in any way, especially since neither of them could speak English. They were both assigned seats in the last row of First-Class, while he was seated directly behind them, on the aisle in the first row of Coach, so that he could be close to them if needed. Then he told me the most important thing of all:

"*They cannot be spoken to by any woman.* Please be sure to tell the flight attendants this."

I assured him that I would do so and proceeded with my other duties involving the busy flight. I then forgot all about his last words.

Once boarding began, the devotee accompanied them and everyone took their assigned seats, per normal.

Then, the international incident occurred. The First-Class flight attendant, as a part of her normal pre-departure duties, approached the two saffron-garbed gentlemen. She SPOKE to them, asking if they'd like something to drink before takeoff. Worse off, she had TOUCHED one on the shoulder as she asked.

HORRORS!

As I understood later, things happened in the blink of an eye. First, both religious leaders looked truly furious at these spoken words, and one actually brushed the flight attendants arm away. Secondly, the devotee rushed up from his coach seat and quickly calmed the two men.

Then he turned to the flight attendant, who was practically in tears, and explained and apologized for the entire situation.

"Didn't the gate agent tell you not to say one word to these people?" he asked.

Meanwhile, back in the gatehouse, I was completely unaware of what had happened until I went back on to dispatch the flight. With just one scathing look from the First-Class flight attendant, I knew I was in trouble. Unfortunately, it was only then that I recalled the stern warning I'd been given – then forgotten – by the devotee. Truth be known, I had not said a word about her not saying a word.

THE PAIN WAS PLAIN

It started out to be a normal day, but that would soon change. A flight had arrived from Atlanta. The passengers had deplaned and now it was about 45 minutes till the plane was to leave again, using the same flight crew that had come in. I went on board to bring the flight attendants some pre-flight paperwork. It was then that they told me the ominous news: Barry, who was their A-Line, (the leading attendant on that crew) was not feeling well and, in fact, they were worried about him. Fortunately, we did have a reserve flight attendant on hand who could quickly fill in if just such a situation occurred. I needed to talk with Barry about his condition right away. Soon enough, I spotted him making his way towards the gate, extremely slowly. In fact, he was almost staggering. I quickly approached him and asked how he was doing.

"Terrible"

Did he want me to get a reserve flight attendant to take his place?

"Absolutely! I feel just awful, man"

Within moments I made the call to have the reserve attendant take his place. Then I turned my attention to Barry who had now collapsed into one of the gatehouse chairs. He looked pretty bad, perspiring profusely and in obvious pain.

Then he began to groan. Feeling alarmed, I asked him if I should call the paramedics.

"Please do" he said, as he clutched at his stomach.

I called for the O'Hare paramedics. Meanwhile, Barry's groans became louder and louder. The guy was really hurting. As the minutes ticked by, Barry began YELLING OUT LOUD. Unfortunately, he was yelling out the F-word and the S-word, almost at the top of his lungs. People nearby were getting scared, and passengers walking down the hall were being startled.

With each passing moment, his ear-splitting swearing became even more intense, to the point that they were almost screams. I had to do something.

I sat down next to Barry and told him the paramedics were on the way. I told him, most sincerely, that I realized he was in a lot of discomfort.

Meanwhile, the sweat was pouring off him, his eyes were bulging, and he was contorting his torso in a rictus of pain. But, as a Delta PSA, I was expected to do my best to create calm out of stressful situations. So, embracing this responsibility, I also told him that his screams were *scaring* the other passengers, especially with his use of those two bad words. Then I simply asked him to substitute "fudge" for the f-word, and "sugar" for the s-word whenever he felt another scream coming on. He looked at me incredulously.

My calming suggestion worked! But, only once or twice. It became crystal clear that for Barry, bellowing "SUGAR and "FUDGE!" just didn't relieve his agony nearly as well.

Eventually the paramedics came and carried him away on a stretcher, still screaming the words I cannot print. Needless to say, all of us were worried about just what terrible medical issue he had been suffering. It turned out that it was a kidney stone! I've been told that the pain of kidney stones can be worse than that of childbirth. Poor Barry was released from the hospital the next day and spent a week recovering at home.

Days later, I painfully cracked my shin against a gatehouse chair. There was no one else around. I'm not afraid to admit that a very loud word instantly sprang from my own responsible lips. It wasn't "sugar!"

ARRIVAL DELAY

As the first inbound flight of the day landed just after 6:30, an experienced Gate PSA went down the jetway to meet the plane. It was a warm morning, and the skies were just starting to brighten. Because of airport congestion, it took much longer than usual for the Delta plane to taxi into the ramp area. Eventually, passengers watched from the airplane's windows, as well as from the windows of the gate house, as it smoothly pulled into the gate and then stopped, awaiting its connection with the jet bridge. However, the bridge didn't move a bit. This was not terribly rare; sometimes there were brief electrical issues which were solved by the ramp personnel, usually just by flipping a circuit-breaker. Other problems needed an experienced mechanic to solve, and these could take longer, much to the ire of the incoming passengers. However, in this instance, there were no calls for help at all, and this was exceedingly strange. Several minutes passed when, finally, the captain contacted the Delta Operations Center at O'Hare and asked what the problem was. He could clearly see the PSA standing in the jetway. The ticket agents at that gate then got a call from the Operations Center, asking why the passengers still hadn't deplaned. So, at this point, one of them went down the jetway himself to see what the matter was. There he found the PSA, leaning against the wall with his head down. He was fast asleep!

PERFECT TIMING

Throughout my years at Delta Air Lines, I always felt that it was a company that truly tried to maintain a "family" type of relationship with their customers, and even more so with their dedicated employees. An example of that occurred when I celebrated my twentieth anniversary with Delta. From across the entire system, those of us who were celebrating a similar anniversary that month were all invited to Atlanta for a special commemorative luncheon. It was quite fancy, and each table was covered with white tablecloths, highlighting the fresh, red roses that made up the centerpieces. Each of us had a name tag next to our assigned places. Upon sitting down, we noticed that, also next to our places, there were boxes of new, gold-colored watches. Much to our amazement, each watch *had already been set to the correct time zone of its recipient.* I thought that was so cool! As the meal progressed, our waitress was quite friendly. She was also older than most of us and, at times, seemed to struggle a bit with handling plates that were heavily laden with food. It was only after the luncheon ended that I found out that she wasn't a trained waitress at all. In fact, she was a salaried Delta employee, who also happened to be the Station Manager of Greensboro. In fact, all of the "waitresses" and "waiters" that served us that day were Station Managers or even higher, including Vice Presidents. This tradition was a long-standing one, and it was something each of the servers happily volunteered for, year after year. They loved it as much as we did. What a special memory!

O'HARE TRIVIA PAGE 2

In the more recent past, the deafening sound of aircraft at O'Hare was also accompanied by roars of a different kind: the roaring of souped-up cars coming from a racetrack located near Manheim and Irving Park roads. It was called the O'Hare Stadium and the automobile races there were a popular attraction from 1956 to 1968. I had the chance to speak with a man who was one of the top drivers in that era, and he gave me a copy of the picture below, showing the car he drove. Not nearly as fast as a jet plane but almost as loud.

WEAPONIZED

From time to time, Delta public contact employees at the airport were required to test the proficiency of the TSA personnel at the entrance to the concourse, particularly regarding their response to suspicious objects shown on the Xray machine. Therefore, once or twice a week, one of us would try to "sneak" through a questionable item. We had different things to use in this ploy, and one was a pistol-shaped object made of metal. There also was a lead pipe and a fake, iron hand grenade. I'll never forget the day I volunteered to be the security checker. I chose the gun. Therefore, that morning I approached the security checkpoint in my normal manner, lunchbox in hand, smiling at the TSA folks who all knew me on sight. However, hidden in my SOCK, I had cleverly placed the gun, nestled completely beside my ankle. On the other hand, though I wanted to appear as innocent as possible, if anyone had looked at me closely, they would have seen all the signs of a very nervous, bad guy. Even though the gun was fake, and I knew the entire exercise was a drill, I was totally stressed. Even *pretending* to be a criminal was nerve-wracking. My heart was racing, I was sweating profusely and the smile I thought I was wearing was surely more of a grimace. Nevertheless, approaching the concourse check point, I placed my lunchbox on the conveyor belt and nonchalantly walked through the magnetometer.

BEEP!

"Hmmm," I said, trying to appear calm, cool and collected. "Must have been something in my lunchbox." I was instructed to walk through again.

BEEP! BEEP!

At this point I needed to be body-searched. I suspect it was more difficult to examine the area around my chest because my heart was pounding so furiously. Eventually the searching hands made their way down to my feet and discovered the weapon I had hidden there. I WAS CAUGHT! Frankly, I was relieved but at the same time happy, that the TSA employees had again done their job perfectly. Furthermore, that "hidden" weapon hadn't gotten any of them (or me) in trouble. Whew!

GRANDFATHERS

A man checked in with me one day at O'Hare, and I noticed that his name was Richard Mudd. Just out of curiosity, I asked him if he was related to the famous (or infamous) Samuel Mudd. He was Samuel's grandson! We had a short conversation about the history surrounding his grandfather. You may recall that Samuel Mudd was the doctor who treated John Wilkes Booth, who had badly injured his leg during his escape from the assassination of Abraham Lincoln. Dr. Mudd was arrested, charged with conspiracy and sentenced to prison at Fort Jefferson. There he eventually became the prison's doctor and was instrumental in stemming an outbreak of yellow fever, tirelessly saving many lives. Because of this, his jail sentence was pardoned, and he lived the rest of his life on his family farm in Maryland. However, his conviction for conspiracy was never overturned. In fact, at O'Hare that day Richard, told me that his family was still involved in petitioning the government to get that conviction overturned. They were unsuccessful. By the way, the phrase, "Your name will be Mudd" is often associated with Dr. Samuel Mudd, but its initial usage preceded Mudd's birth by many years. Even today there is some debate about just how big a role Samuel Mudd played in the conspiracy to kill President Lincoln. Sadly, the conviction can never be overturned, as too much time has passed since that initial conviction occurred. Samuel's name will always be Mudd.

I met another grandson – or perhaps great grandson – one day. His name was John Phillip Sousa III. As with Mudd, we had a nice conversation about the <u>original</u> John P. Sousa. His grandson was still in possession of the desk that was used during the creation of many of Sousa's well-known marching songs. He also had several original pieces of sheet music. I enjoyed meeting him immensely but restrained myself from whistling "Stars and Stripes Forever" until he had departed. Unfortunately, he told me that there wouldn't be *another* John P. Sousa to carry on that hallowed name. He had no brothers, was single and was quite certain that he'd never father a IV edition.

BALLS

The Boston Celtics were flying on Delta from O'Hare to Atlanta, and I was assigned to work their flight. Shortly before boarding, I asked Kevin McHale to tell me the name of the team's equipment manager, and if the manager had a good sense of humor. He said he did. So, I paged the unsuspecting man to the gate podium. "Sir," I said, "I've just received a call from our baggage facility. Your team, I believe, was traveling with several large 'Celtics' duffel bags. Is that correct?"

"Yes"

"Unfortunately, two of the larger bags got terribly jammed up in our conveyor system. One appeared to have contained basketballs, the other several uniforms. Both duffel bags were destroyed. Most of the basketballs literally *popped* under the pressure, and many uniforms became torn and covered with oil. I am terribly sorry to tell you this, but just stop into our baggage service office in Atlanta, and we can process any compensation."

The man was aghast. "What? What? "How could such a thing ever happen?" "We need those balls and uniforms for our evening game in Atlanta!" McHale – and others on the team – were listening to our exchange, carefully keeping the grins off their faces. The equipment manager continued, getting more and more flustered. "This is just ridiculous! I don't know what we're going to do!"

I simply paused for a moment...took a deep breath...and then grinned!

Slowly it dawned on him that the entire episode was a practical joke, and that McHale and the others were totally in on it.

I can't repeat the choice words he said to me at that point, nor the exasperated looks he gave towards the rest of the team, most of whom were chuckling good-naturedly. But, indeed, all was well with the Boston Celtics baggage, and they went on to beat Atlanta that night. I like to think that when they first took the floor, many of them remembered the events of the morning and played with some extra smiles, all pointed in the direction of their poor manager.

BEING NEEDLED

When I was a wee lad, I was anemic. In fact, I was so badly anemic that by age two, I needed regular shots of iron to keep my red blood count normal. My mom would DRAG me down the street, kicking and screaming, to the nearby doctor's office, where he'd inject me with iron. That shot really hurt too, especially because it was put directly into my tender little butt. I've never forgotten that evil doctor's name, either. It was "Tessus."

Years later, working for Delta at O'Hare, a man strolled up to my desk and showed me his boarding pass.

OMG! The name on the pass was "Tessus." I recoiled in horror.

"What? What? Is there something wrong?" the man asked, wonderingly.

I replied that "Tessus" was not a very pleasant name for me. Then, I proceeded to tell him the whole sad story.

The man directly in front of me was the *son* of my boyhood scourge: the evil Dr. Tessus!

He was surprisingly sympathetic to my story and shared with me the fact that he and his brother used to laugh at the little kids who screamed and cried when they came to their dad's office for shots. Accordingly, one day, Dr. Tessus brought both of his boys into his office and administered harmless, saline injections into *their* rear ends, just so they'd be more sympathetic. They never laughed at a child's tears again, and one of the brothers went on to become a doctor himself. In fact, it was the same man who was now talking with me at the airport.

This time, my story with the nice Dr. Tessus had a happy ending – no ifs, ands, nor *butts* about it!

DAVE

During my tenure as gate PSA, I worked side by side with many fellow Red Coats. One of them was named Dave Segmuth. Dave was a truly personable guy, quiet, intelligent and perfectly calm, even amidst angry passengers or long flight delays. He and I were a great team.

One day an arriving passenger, whom I recognized as a frequent flyer, came up to me and said, "Jeff, I saw this in Atlanta and knew I had to get it for you." It looked a lot like a camera, but it was *made out of rubber.* Moreover, it wasn't a camera at all, but, in fact, was a cleverly disguised squirt gun! The passenger demonstrated how it worked: just aim and squeeze. Simple.

I couldn't wait to try it out, and within minutes filled it with water from a nearby drinking fountain. At that moment, Dave Segmuth came walking by.

"Hey Dave," I said, "Let me take your picture."

Quickly I approached him. Meanwhile, Dave straightened himself up, smiled, and assumed a professional pose. Getting close, I pointed the rubber camera at his chest, compressed it firmly and watched with glee as a stream of water was propelled directly onto his red PSA jacket. Ha!

It was then that I encountered a side of Dave never seen before. He was furious! He was so mad I thought he was going to punch my lights out. Even the Hulk couldn't have looked more fearsome at that point. And never, ever, did I think he was capable of such absolute anger. I can't repeat the epithets he yelled in my direction. Suddenly, it didn't seem so funny anymore, and I apologized profusely, feeling awful.

I'm happy to say that our friendship survived this ordeal, and life went on as normal. The thought of revenge never appeared to have entered his mind.

Many weeks later, Dave asked me what the initial "O" stood for in my name. (Jeffrey O. Degner)

I told him, "Owen"

"Oh wow" said Dave, "I really, really like that name!"

"Thanks, Dave. I've become attached to it myself"

Eventually, Dave transferred to San Francisco, and it was years before I saw him again, striding down the concourse in my direction.

"Hello, Dave Segmuth!" I called out.

He stopped, came up to my desk with a smile and then said, "I'm not Dave Segmuth anymore. I've officially changed my last name. It only cost $75.00, too"

"What's your new last name?"

"It's Owen. I'm now Dave Owen!"

Holy Moly! Did he name himself after me? I didn't want to ask, but I certainly think it was a possibility. Don't you? Would you like to rename yourself too? I would truly be honored - again!

MUSICAL CHAIRS

In the 1970s, a popular passenger jet used by Delta was the DC9. There actually were **two** versions of the DC9 flying in and out of O'Hare. One, the most common, was a "Regular 9" whose seating arrangements included 12 First-Class seats. The other was a "Baby 9" This plane, though smaller in its overall dimensions, had 24 First-Class seats. Unfortunately, there was one instance when the wrong kind of DC9 had been loaded into the Delta reservation system, The gate agents working the flight on that fateful day, never realized it until First Class boarding had begun. Thus it was, that 24 First Class passengers were trying to find space for themselves in a cabin with just twelve seats. Oh, oh! As the PSA responsible for that flight, I received a frantic call from the gate agents. Soon, I faced 12 angry, completely seatless customers. An unspoken rule at the time was that First-Class seats were never taken from a customer. A flight might be late...meals denied...baggage lost...any of these misfortunes paled as compared with the passenger being advised of an "Involuntary Downgrade." Here I was, in front of 12 of them.

I went on board and asked everyone in First Class to deplane. Amidst grumbles and groans, they all did so. Then I explained the situation and allowed the folks whose seats matched those in the front cabin to reboard.

For those unhappy customers still waiting, I had several options which I announced in order.

1: Try to arrange an "equipment substitution" and get the right sized plane. (This was a *total ruse* – I knew I could never make this happen)

"NO!" they all said.

2: Put them all in First Class on later flights.

"NO!" they all said. "NO WAY!"

3: Arrange comfortable seating in coach class for everyone with appropriate refunds. Surprisingly, there <u>still</u> were a lot of angry or unhappy faces.

4: Arrange comfortable seating in coach class for everyone with appropriate refunds and <u>free drinks</u>. Voila! This solved the problem. Everyone accepted a reassigned seat in the second cabin, and the flight left on time. Mission accomplished – without playing musical chairs!

O'HARE TRIVIA PAGE 3

In the 1970s, a nudist colony/adult entertainment complex in Indiana was owned and operated by a charismatic Chicagoan named Dick Drost. He even had his own plane, a "de Havilland Comet", in which folks could fly to his resort, called "Naked City." One trip to O'Hare, sadly, would be the last one his plane would ever make. His unique airplane never received the proper takeoff authorizations. So, the Naked City Comet was towed to a remote area just off a main taxiway, awaiting the appropriate paperwork. It sat there, in full view of the public, for years, while it slowly deteriorated. Its tires flattened, its windshield broke, and birds and small animals made it their home. Mr. Drost passed away, but the plane remained. Finally, it turned out that this type of aircraft had become a rarity! A vintage airplane organization paid to have it removed and completely restored to its former glory. It now sits in proud display at an antique aircraft museum. The nudist colony closed in 1986.

COAT TALE

At O'Hare, as well as at most airports, there are occasional public-address announcements pertaining to not leaving your personal belongings unattended, as well as about notifying authorities when observing any unattended or suspicious items. I've been on both sides of that coin.

It was a cold day in January, and standing out in the frigid jetways, we gate agents needed to wear heavy coats when we met and dispatched the flights. My own coat was a super-warm, Delta parka. After leaving the jetway on one occasion that morning, I hung my parka up in the gatehouse coat rack and went about my inside business. My assigned gate had two boarding doors, far apart from each other.

While I was temporarily stationed in front of door 8B, I could clearly see, in the distance, the area around door 8A, including the coat rack where my parka was hung. As time went on, I just happened to notice a man get up from his seat near me at 8B and take another seat closer to 8A. I assumed that this was where his own flight would be boarding. His new gatehouse seat ended up directly below the coat rack. Suddenly, to my amazement, he reached up into that rack and knocked my parka to the floor! Then, after a few minutes, (as I continued watching in disbelief) he nonchalantly scooped it up and *stuffed it into his carry-on bag.*

He was stealing my nice, warm coat, literally in front of my eyes. I was furious!

Somehow, I kept myself from confronting the thief and so, first, I told my supervisor, Ron, about it. He could see how angry I was. I wanted to call the police, have the man arrested and spend years in jail, after breaking all his fingers, of course. Who knows what else he'd stolen from innocent people just like me? My supervisor, though, took a much calmer approach.

Ron and I both walked up to the man, where I emphatically declared, "YOU'VE GOT MY COAT IN YOUR BAG!"

The man said, "Oh, really? Is this yours? I saw it on the floor and put it inside my bag to take to the airport lost-and-found department. Sorry!"

The dirty rat was lying through his teeth, of course. But after that, I always kept my personal belongings much closer and never unattended, just like those frequent airport announcements tell everyone to do – including airline employees.

FLOPPED

It was ten minutes before departure when I went on the busy
flight and gave the final paperwork to the flight attendants and
pilots. That's when Debbie, the "A-Line" flight attendant told
me that there was an ill passenger on board, traveling with her
spouse, and both wanted to deplane. As we spoke, I saw the
couple making their way towards me in the front of the plane.
The woman was moving slowly but surely, holding her
husband's arm. I spoke with them briefly and concluded that
it indeed would be best for them to go later. At that time, the
woman slumped a little, and I suggested we all leave the plane
together. She slumped a little more, so while her spouse took
one of her arms, putting it behind his neck and over his
shoulder, I did the same with the other, both of us providing
the support she needed to continue walking. Then she passed
out completely! The only thing holding her up were the two of
us. We looked at each other and said, "Uh-oh"

She was a larger woman and staggering with her weight, we
were able to get her out of the plane, whereupon we gently laid
her on the jetway floor. Over the radio, I'd already called for the
O'Hare paramedics. Then I noticed that we had positioned with
her head facing *down* the steep jetway rather than up.
Consequently, her legs had flopped open, along with her skirt,

and it wasn't a very pretty view. Her husband quickly rearranged things as she lay comatose. It was now departure time.

I closed the door of the plane and approached the jetway controls to back the jet bridge off the aircraft. That's when I noticed that we'd unfortunately repositioned the poor woman directly on top of one of the telescoping sections of the jetway. As it retracted, it would be retracting <u>directly under her</u>! Who knows what that could have done to her back or legs?

Therefore, hubby and I grabbed her legs and dragged her off that dangerous area, sliding her a brief distance into a safer location. This was hard work! I pulled the jetway away and just a few minutes later the paramedics arrived. Hurray!

After checking her vital signs, the ambulance team immediately gave her oxygen. Seconds later, her eyes fluttered open, and within just a few minutes she was perfectly fine. As it turned out, it was the start of their honeymoon, and she and her new husband were heading to Jamaica. They'd had a raucous wedding reception, and both had overindulged a little. She also had been sleepless most of that previous night, full of excitement about their upcoming trip together. Furthermore, she'd never been on a flight before! All these factors combined to bring out a serious case of dehydration, and it is this that caused her collapse. With a prompt intake of fluids, she was given the okay to go home. I was delighted to see them both the next day. She looked wonderful: a much better way to start their marriage.

SENIOR MOMENTS

An elderly lady was flying alone and standing by as a "non-rev" for a busy flight I was working one day. She was the parent of a Delta employee, and her standby priority was low. Though I could see that the seats were filling up, I still thought she had a good chance of getting on. Furthermore, noticing how worried she looked I kept leaving my desk and trying to reassure her. As it turned out, she got one of the last seats on the flight – and it was in First-Class! When I handed the boarding card to her, she said, "You know, Mr. Degner, I'm 93 years old. I'm not sure how many more trips I have ahead of me. But I'll ALWAYS remember this! Thank you"

On another flight, another day, another senior citizen "needed assistance," according to her reservation data. Usually, this meant the use of a wheelchair, or sometimes just a strong arm, to help a passenger get from the gatehouse to the aircraft. She seemed bright and energetic, though, so I approached her with this statement, "Hi Mrs. Brinkman. We now have two different ways that we can help you get onto the plane. One is the traditional wheelchair method. The other is our new, 'pull-and-drag" method.

She asked about the pull-and-drag method.

"We grab you by the back of your shirt and pull and drag you onto the plane!"

She replied with a big grin, "Let's go with the pull and drag method, you brute!"

I was accepting and scanning boarding cards at the jetway door one day, while simultaneously chatting with a flight attendant I knew. As one passenger approached, probably in her eighties, I noticed that she was pulling a collapsible luggage cart. On it were a typical tote bag and above that bag was a picnic-basket type of container, like the one Dorothy used in "The Wizard of Oz". As she proceeded past the two of us, one of the flaps in that picnic basket opened up a bit. Out popped the head of a little dog who looked around and made a tiny "Yip" sound! The woman looked mortified and quickly closed the flap, putting a book on top of it and looking at me nervously. I let her pass without comment. Then I said to the flight attendant, "I didn't see a thing, did you?" "Nope. I didn't hear anything either!" End of story.

STUCK IT!

In my younger years, I played a lot of racquetball. I was known for my ability to DIVE for balls that otherwise seemed unreachable. In my mind, the dives were swan-like things of poise and beauty. To my opponents, they more often resembled painful belly flops. Nevertheless, the technique was a successful one, and I scored many a point by its unexpected use. One day in the gatehouse, I was hustling from the desk to the boarding door. Unfortunately, I didn't notice that a passenger's carry-on bag had just been placed in the direction I was striding. I didn't see it at all, tripped, and at that moment I knew I was going down. Realizing this, I instinctively went into my famous racquetball diving mode. I flew through the air like an eagle, landed hard, but then turned the landing into a front-roll summersault and popped up, unhurt and smiling. There were gasps throughout the gatehouse and a moment of complete silence while all the passengers realized what an Olympic-style floor routine they had just witnessed. I gave myself a 9 for difficulty and a 9.5 for execution. Then I nonchalantly returned to the desk as I imagined hearing the shouts of, "USA! USA! USA!"

O'HARE TRIVIA PAGE 4

Is Chicago's O'Hare International Airport the busiest airport in the United States? Not anymore! For many years it held that honor, but in 1998 it was ousted by Atlanta's Hartsfield-Jackson. More recently it has dropped into third place, after Los Angeles. By the way, in the late 40's and early 50's, another Chicago airport was the busiest in the country: Midway. However, Midway's shorter runways eventually could not accommodate the larger jets, such as the Boeing 707 whose takeoffs and landings required much more room. Boxed in completely by neighborhoods, Midway simply could not expand to meet those demands.

In the early 1970's, O'Hare's five story parking garage was the largest such structure in the world.

The next time you're at O'Hare, look closely at the upper windows of the United terminal. It was a state-of-the-art facility designed by Helmut Jahn, completed in 1988. Unfortunately, the original windows were slanted in such a way that at certain times of the day they reflected blinding sunlight into the eyes of the O'Hare control tower operators! Consequently, at the cost of thousands and thousands of dollars, the windows were all etched gray, and the problem no longer exists.

THE LONG SHOT

In the first two decades that I worked for Delta I played a lot of 12"' softball. I was a member of our local ORD (O'Hare) Delta team and the year we won the O'Hare league championship we then also flew to Tampa to take part in a *national* airline tournament. This was real, big-time softball. The field was perfect. Hundreds, if not thousands of folks were in the stands, and there even was an enthusiastic announcer. I clearly remember the first time I got up to the plate, hearing over the field's P.A. speakers: "Now at bat is First Baseman, Jeff Degner." Oh, how exciting! That first at-bat is forever etched in my memory. I hit the ball a long way, and I knew, with my blinding speed, it was certainly a double, if not a triple. But then, as I raced around first base and headed towards second, the unthinkable happened. A vicious, Florida wasp flew into my open shirt and became trapped between it and my heaving chest. OMG! I certainly did not want to be stung. So, running towards second, I ripped that uniform jersey right off my head, then stopped abruptly, shook it out furiously, and abandoned all thoughts of continuing to third. The wasp flew out, perhaps heading for the next base itself. I don't recall what the announcer said, witnessing this unique display. I also wonder what the spectators thought! And, frankly, I recall little else about the tournament, other than the white seagulls which constantly had to be chased off the green ball field. But I'll never forget my first big-time at-bat in the only national tournament I've ever played in.

Besides the Delta softball team, I also played in a local league with two of my brothers. Indeed, there were <u>three</u> Degner brothers on the same team, and we loved playing together over many years. Unfortunately, there were three *other* brothers on a different team – the "Smith" brothers and they became our softball nemeses.

The Degner team and the Smith team had many an emotional game against each other, each one more volatile than the previous. In fact, there was one instance when I was so furious with Tom Smith that we had to be physically restrained from an outright fist fight.

As time went on, though, the Smith brothers retired from softball. Tom Smith became a paramedic in town while his brother, Tim, became a firefighter. We Degner brothers continued playing for several more years, often practicing on the high school field. On occasion, an ambulance might drive by – even a fire truck – and one of the two Smith brothers might lay on the horn and yell, "DEGNER!" as they passed by. Year by year, the old rivalry and anger towards each other seemed to pass. Or so I thought.

While on the job at O'Hare one day, I badly injured my hand, cutting myself with a piece of metal and causing a deep, bloody wound. Unable to continue working, I was able to temporarily wrap it with tissues and tape, and I drove myself to the hospital in town. Ow! At the emergency room, it was determined that I'd need a tetanus shot as a part of the treatment. I hated injections of any kind and waited nervously behind the screening in a private cubicle. Within minutes, the curtains slowly parted and in walked paramedic **Tom Smith**! My worst nightmare! I had no idea that our local paramedics were required to spend time in active hospital settings. So, there was Tom Smith. And in his hand was one, HUGE hypodermic syringe. He looked at m…and smiling like the devil himself, said "DEGNER!"

Tom was both gentle and professional as he administered that injection. It hardly hurt at all. From that moment on, each time we saw each other in town we'd both smile, shake hands warmly and talk about how our various brothers were doing. Somehow, the subject of softball never came up again.

JETWAY SHOWER

When Delta Gate Agents dispatched a flight, there were certain procedures that we always followed. We'd present the flight attendant and pilots with any final paperwork, make a welcoming on-board announcement, close the door of the plane, then step back into the jetway's control panel area, watch out the window for a ramp guide-person and slowly pull the jetway from the plane. Personally, I liked to stand at the end of that jetway once it was detached, and watch the plane back out, often saluting a goodbye to the pilots. Lastly, we'd close the outside door of the jetway. These outer, weather doors kept rain, sleet and snow from entering the main part of the jet bridge.

Glycol is a slippery, odorous, red-colored, de-icing substance which is sprayed vigorously on the wings and fuselages of planes when certain freezing weather conditions are met. The glycol often comes from powerful hoses manned by ramp employees in "cherry-picker" vehicles, high above or to the side of the planes. This is done to prevent a buildup of ice on the aircraft which could be critical during takeoff.

One winter day in late December, our new department head, Rob came to the gate area to witness our operation there. Normally he'd be in his office behind the ticket counter attending to important managerial Issues all day long. However, on this particular day, one of his first since being promoted to manager, Rob really wanted to immerse himself in our gate operation.

I was about to dispatch a flight when Rob, dressed in a snazzy, bright green sport jacket, came up to me and said, "I'll go with you!" So, Rob and I went down the jetway. He watched closely while I went about the normal dispatch procedures, almost as if he was assessing my performance.

After pulling the jetway off the plane, Rob said, "You can go back to the gate. I'll stay here till the plane backs out."

I forgot to remind him about the glycol spraying which was taking place that cold day.

Unfortunately, I also neglected to tell him to close the weather door.

A few minutes later, Rob walked back into the gatehouse and softly closed the jetway door behind him. He was literally DRIPPING with glycol. It was in his hair, on his trousers and shoes and there were splotches of it all over his nice, green jacket. He was a <u>very</u> unhappy man. I wanted to point out that the red splotches on his green jacket nicely matched the Christmas colors that were present throughout the airport. However, this was clearly not the time for my famous sense of humor, so I simply watched as he slowly left the area, leaving little red puddles of glycol behind. That green jacket was never the same.

SCARRED

In my first book, *What track for the Atlanta Flight*, I described some unfortunate instances where I was physically assaulted by angry or drunk passengers. During my long career, these events were quite rare, but they included being choked, slugged, spritzed with perfume and grabbed by my hair. None of them, however, come close to how frightened I was on one memorable night.

We were short-handed and I was alone, working a 9:00PM flight on a busy evening, directly across the hall from another Delta gate. My desk phone rang; it was someone at our ticket counter warning me to be on the lookout for a customer who appeared to be intoxicated.

Sure enough, within a few minutes, I saw a young woman in her early 20s walking towards me. More accurately, she was *staggering* towards the gate. I'll just call her "Ponytail." She came up to me, leaned against the desk and fumbled in her purse to find her boarding pass. Her breath stank of alcohol. Taking her pass, I asked her to have a seat in the gatehouse. It was clear to me that she was too inebriated to fly. Consequently, when I had the chance, I sat down next to her and told her that because of her condition, I'd be booking her on a different flight. Ponytail was furious, screaming at me and shouting that she was perfectly fine. Eventually, she left the gate. I was relieved.

However, my joy was short lived. Ponytail came back, *now accompanied by her three brothers*, who had come to the airport to see her off. This was before 9-11 and anyone could enter the concourse. Two of her three brothers were huge and looked like linebackers for a professional football team. The third was smaller but had a vicious scar across his face. All three of them were extremely angry with me and my decision not to allow Ponytail on the flight.

They came closer and closer, and the smaller one said they were going to beat the sh*t out of me. He also promised that I'd soon have a scar just like his. Frankly, I don't recall what I said at that exact moment, but whatever it was, seemed to calm them down a bit. They finally decided that they would not hurt me and left the area with their sister in tow. Whew!

Then they changed their minds.

Within three minutes, the entire group was back again and, by the menacing looks on their faces, I knew I was in trouble. I distinctly remember shrugging off my uniform jacket to be able to move more easily. I also stepped away from behind the desk to avoid being trapped there. At the time, each Delta gate position also contained a pneumatic tube system, with which we sent paper documents back and forth. The tubes themselves were about 10 inches long, heavy and virtually indestructible. Before leaving the desk area, I grabbed one of them for self-defense, and now directly faced the irate men about to attack me. Time stood still.

Somehow, though, I had lost sight of one of them. He had circled around *behind* me!

There is a wrestling hold called a "Full Nelson." In it, the attacker, standing behind his opponent, places both of his arms under the arms and shoulders of the other, then clasps both hands tightly behind their neck, immobilizing the arms and pushing the victim's head down with tremendous force.

OMG, this is exactly what happened to me. My arms were now useless, and I weakly dropped the pneumatic tube to the floor. As this entire incident was unfolding, the gate agent across the hall had called the police. Suddenly, a middle-aged lady walking by also saw what was happening and cried out, "Leave him alone! Leave him alone!" Hearing this, Ponytail went up to the lady and SLAPPED her across the face!

My would-be helper burst into tears and ran away. So, there I was, arms useless, staring at three angry men who were about to make good on their threats of beating me to a pulp and leaving me scarred forever.

What could I do?

What would you do?

What I did was...apologize. Even though, truly, I had nothing to regret, it seemed like the only thing I had left to try. I said to them, "Ok. I'm sorry. I think you may be right. I'm going to get her back on the flight. Give me a minute to make it happen."

Truth be known, I was simply stalling for time. I had no intention of letting Ponytail on board. But my ploy stopped their planned violence. The one who still held my arms in a vice-like grip said, "*Now* you're talking, a**hole. Make it happen."

At that exact moment, several members of the O'Hare police department approached the gate. I was saved! They confronted the brothers whose demeanor had instantly changed to one of peace and tranquility.

"We're just having a friendly discussion with this nice Delta agent." they said. "We'll be on our way now."

The policemen saw this as an acceptable solution to the entire incident, and, with Ponytail and her three brothers, proceeded to walk towards the airport exit. However, first, Scarface stopped in front of me. Looking me in the eye, and flashing a throat-cutting gesture, he said, most ominously, "We'll be waiting for you"

True to his word, hour after hour, that furious group waited at the end of the concourse for me to finish work. I had Delta scouts giving me regular updates: "They're still there!" until it was finally time for me to leave. Even then, the brothers, along with Ponytail, had continued to maintain their vigil.

As luck would have it on this particular day, I had not parked in our regular Delta employee lot. In fact, I'd been running late to work, and simply drove into the public garage adjacent to the terminal.

With this in mind, I decided to exit the concourse *one level lower*, via the ramp area normally used for service employees and baggage carts. By doing this, I completely bypassed the volatile group still waiting for me above on the regular airport concourse, or so I hoped.

Stepping out of a door in the baggage-claim area, I walked across to the parking garage and to my car. It was dark and lonely in that big building, and to say the least, that short journey was pretty nerve wracking. I regretted not asking someone to keep me company. But I made it to my car with no problems, other than my pounding heart, and gratefully drove home. I never saw the brothers again. Even now, though, I'm amazed at how this sequence of events played out, and especially, how fortunate I had been. It remains the worst customer memory of my career.

HUMOR ON THE JOB

Working as a gate agent can be an incredibly stressful and hectic job, especially when there are flight delays or rude passengers. For me, the use of humor was a great way to defuse many a bad situation, or to just provide brief moments of levity for both myself and my (usually) appreciative passengers and colleagues. Amidst some of the busiest days ever, I still often found a way to just...have fun. And I did this for 45 years! Over the course of those years, here are examples of some of the smile-causing anecdotes for which I became famous.

One Halloween I brought a gray, rubber mouse to work. Dangling it by its tail, I approached Kim, one of my fellow passenger service agents, and slowly tapped her on the back. She turned, saw the mouse and SHRIEKED! Ha! This was just the reaction I had hoped for. The following Halloween, I did the same thing with the same rubber mouse. She shrieked again! I *could* have just stopped then. But once more, the very next Halloween, I noticed that Kim was standing in a hallway with three other female agents, all about to enter an employee break room. Repeating my successful procedures of the past two years, I tapped her on the back and dangled that mouse once more. My goodness, she shrieked her loudest this time! But so did every other one of the women standing in line, *even though they didn't see the mouse.* They only screamed because Kim screamed. What fun!

On flights which were practically empty, I'd make unusual announcements. A common example was, "Anyone wearing a babushka may board early." Most of the passengers didn't know what a babushka was. But occasionally there was someone who did, often improvising with a scarf, then sashaying on board, smiling all the while. There were other instances when I'd offer early boarding to people *wearing glasses.* One man tried to sneak on board when he clearly wasn't wearing any. Of course, I stopped him sternly. He slowly pointed to his eyes and said, "contacts!" and proudly walked on. Once a flight only had 9 booked passengers. Looking around, I offered pre-boarding to anyone wearing blue shoes. With that, a teenage girl looked down at her feet and practically *skipped* down the jetway, ahead of her bemused parents. Another favorite announcement of mine was to tell passengers that, to save space for their personal items, I could put a special luggage tag on any of THEIR CHILDREN and check them into the baggage bin. In fact, a former Illinois governor on one of his last public outings before going to jail was booked with his family on a flight I worked. Hearing that exact announcement, he asked me if I could put one of those special bag-tags on his daughter. She thought he was serious!

If I knew that a friend or colleague was arriving on a flight I was meeting, I'd sometimes make a quick on-board announcement, just as the passengers were about to deplane. "May I have your attention please? Illinois law officials have decided to <u>drop all charges</u> against Ms. Fotena Zirps and so it will be okay for Ms. Zirps to deplane in Chicago." Dead silence on the plane usually followed this, while passengers wondered who the pardoned convict was. All they had to do was look for the passenger with the reddest face! Yet another example was, "Attention, arriving passenger John Mahalek, please give twenty dollars to the Delta agent who is meeting this flight." Quite often I'd page "famous" people to the desk, then watch as the folks in the gate house craned their necks to see such celebrities as Brittany Spears, Dennis Rodman, Hillary Rodham, etc. The names changed as the years changed. Early in my career, I even used Mother Theresa.

There was also a way that fictitious reservations could be made, and those faux passengers could then be placed on active standby lists. I loved to do this! Then I'd stroll over to the appropriate gate and listen while the agent carefully paged "Jim Shews," "Paige Turner," or "Ben Dover," etc. The list was a long one. Some agents even fell for the same fake name more than once, paging the passenger several times until spotting me, grinning in the distance. However, the very best example of a comedic name was one that repeatedly fooled gate agents, flight attendants and even pilots: "Mr. Hugh Jass." Ha!

NUTS TO YOU

*This is a **bonus** story, not directly dealing with Delta, O'Hare or Healing the Children! Enjoy!*

I knew a Delta flight attendant, Tammy, who was based in New Orleans. On one of her trips through Chicago, she asked me if I was thinking about returning to Mardi Gras as I had the year before. What a spectacle this celebration is! I fact, I WAS thinking about going back to New Orleans again, (one of the perks of being an airline employee) and I'd be making that trip during one of the busiest weekends of Mardi Gras.

Tammy then told me she'd be riding on one of the floats! In fact, she said, she'd be a part of the huge Zulu parade. Back then, all the float-riders in the Zulu "krewe" (club) wore blackface, a practice which began 100 years ago though recently has become controversial. Furthermore, she said that if we saw each other, she'd be sure to throw me a highly coveted GOLDEN COCONUT. How could I pass this opportunity up?

A few weeks later I found myself on Canal Street in downtown New Orleans, watching the first of the 28 Zulu floats pass by. During Mardi Gras, the float riders toss "throws" to the revelers in the streets. The throws are most often strings of colored beads and mostly worthless. Much less common are "doubloons" which are half-dollar- shaped coins made from tin or aluminum.

They are usually stamped with information such as the date and name of the organization. People jump, run, dive, even tussle on the ground for doubloons and, when caught, hoard them like precious gems. Many are considered collectors' items. However, even more rare than doubloons are the Golden Coconuts for which the Zulu krewe is famous.

Can you imagine the odds that I would see Tammy, who was just one black-faced rider on a float filled with dozens of others? Add to that the frenzy and constant jostling of the crowd as they pushed and shoved for throws. Yet, as float ten passed by, we somehow miraculously saw each other! The crowd on Canal Street was at least six deep, filling the gap between the floats and the sidewalk. Tammy looked at me and I waved, whereupon she reached down…and came up with a Golden Coconut, just for me! Oh, boy! I got to within a few feet of the moving float, and she tossed it to me gently. Only somebody just ahead of me jumped up and intercepted it! There went my chance. But Tammy had another one! This time I got even closer to the float. All I had to do was stretch out my long arms to receive it. She placed it in my hands like a sleeping baby. Much to my surprise, another reveler RIPPED it right out of my hands and scurried away like a dirty rat. I was so disappointed! Yet, one more time, Tammy reached down and came up with another golden coconut.

"The last one" she signaled. This time I got so close to the float that its wheels were literally an inch away from my feet. It was risky for sure, as I shuffled along with the moving 10-ton vehicle. But I WANTED THAT COCONUT! Tammy took the last Golden Coconut and firmly thrust it into my chest. I immediately grabbed it with both hands and tucked it even closer to my body, as if I was receiving a handoff in a football game. Nonetheless, people to the left and right of me still tried to wrestle it from my manly grip! I hung on to it like the treasure it was and slowly retreated to the sidewalk. For the rest of that short day, people offered me money – twenty dollars once – for my Golden Coconut. NEVER!

The Golden Coconut itself was just a regular store-bought coconut that had been painted gold and other colors by the Zulu participants. It really was quite lovely and unique; I could see why they were so much in demand. I was quite proud that I had one, and I just couldn't wait to bring it back.

Later that night, I returned home to triumphantly tell my wife about my golden prize. I had kept it swaddled in my carry-on bag to protect it from any damage. Slowly, to her wondering eyes, I removed it from my bag. "Ta da!" I exclaimed happily. The Golden Coconut now lay exposed in all its glory. Truth be known, it didn't look quite as good as when I first got it. Some of the golden luster had flaked off.

Nevertheless, considering how valuable it was, I soon convinced Marcie that it deserved a special place, to be proudly displayed in our living room. She wasn't all that enthusiastic but succumbed to my joy, and we both placed it in an honorary spot on the mantel shelf above the fireplace. We could clearly see it every day. Yes!

It was less than a week later that Marcie asked me, "What's that strange smell?" We tracked it down to the fireplace mantel. There, to my horror, sat the Golden Coconut, which now had begun to disintegrate. Black ooze was coming out of the bottom, the gold color was almost gone, and it reeked of decay.

Within moments, my prized Golden Coconut was in the garbage can, never to see the light of day again. Sheesh! After all my exertions in New Orleans, I wished I'd taken those twenty dollars for it. Nuts!

PART TWO

Healing the Children
Stories

ESCORTING NEEDY CHILDEN

Some of the most amazing, heartfelt, almost-miraculous experiences I've had with Healing the Children have occurred as I have escorted young people from Central America to Chicago, either alone or with a colleague. I've seen countless mothers, and fathers too, uncontrollably weeping in the airport of their homeland as they handed over to me the child they treasured. Can you imagine the faith they must have to do this, sending a helpless toddler off in the arms of a stranger, about to leave for a faraway land where people don't even speak their language? Furthermore, they know their child could be undergoing painful surgery and recovery without the comfort of their biological *mama* or *papa*.

Many of the poorest children bring very little with them. Yet a modest change of clothes is often in their tattered carry-on bags – plus a roll of toilet paper, which can be a scarce commodity in Nicaragua.

I've also seen countless <u>host</u> mothers and fathers, also crying, as they say goodbye to a child whom they've loved like their own. These departures, though, are bittersweet because that child is now healed, returning to their native home and facing a healthy future.

In addition, several of the insights that I've had with HTC medical missions in Nicaragua and Ecuador have been truly special. They include being in an active operating room, observing firsthand the life-changing surgeries taking place. What a privilege! In most of these missions, the participants usually come from different hospitals and states. Yet, in the setting of the O.R, they effortlessly work as if they'd been with each other for years. All quickly assume their normal duties: physicians, nurses, anesthesiologists, scrub techs, translators. The process is seamless. One Nicaraguan doctor, noting the efficiency of the American surgical team, asked, "How long have you been working together?" The answer was, "Two hours!"

THE STORY OF LORA: A GRANDMOTHER'S LOVE
(First published in *Doing Good for Goodness' Sake* 2004)

Lying limply across her grandmother's lap, the child resembled little more than a rag doll, so still and listless it was hard to tell she was even breathing. Her name was Lora. She was five. To get her to the rural, Nicaraguan hospital, her *abuela* had first carried Lora for four miles, including passing through a swamp where she tenderly held her overhead, keeping her high and dry. Then they traveled for a while on horseback, took a long bus ride, and walked two more miles from the bus station to the hospital. There, the grandmother hoped that a group of Americans could save the life of the fragile girl she'd carried so far.

I was a part of that group, as translator, photographer, and errand-runner. The rest of the members were doctors and nurses who had donated eight days of their time to come to Nicaragua and help as many needy young people as they could. We were doing so under the auspices of the Wisconsin Chapter of the all-volunteer organization called Healing the Children. Word of our impending arrival had been circulating around the Nicaraguan countryside for weeks; several intrepid souls, all seeking some type of medical aid, were even waiting for us in the lobby of our airport hotel.

The next day we set up our clinic in a rambling, one-story hospital outside the town of Rivas. Stray dogs occasionally trotted down the open-air corridors. Hospital laundry hung out to dry in the branches of nearby trees. In the waiting room, which consisted of nothing more than rows of bare, metal, folding chairs, sat dozens and dozens of people. Some, like Lora's grandmother, had journeyed for hours, even days, remaining quiet and patient until their turn to be seen by the American doctors. I would frequently pass through this congested waiting area.

Every time, I'd find myself the focus of all those pairs of dark brown eyes, each one filled with one word: hope.

The medical team brought much of their own equipment with them to Nicaragua. Nevertheless, they also utilized many local items, trying to ignore rusty scalpels, stained, "sterile" gowns and the scorpion eggs found in a cabinet. Potential cases were examined carefully. Some children were promptly scheduled for surgery in the next few days and sent off to wait some more in overcrowded wards without air conditioning. There were no complaints. Others, the most difficult cases, could only be helped back in the United States and thus were put on a different waiting list. Tragically, there were also those who could never be helped. Nicaraguan doctors and nurses worked right alongside the Americans, both as pupils and as able assistants. By the end of their stay, more than 300 children had been seen and 45 different surgeries performed.

Many of the operations involved facial plastic surgery: removal of tumors, repair of cleft lips and palates. A Nicaraguan mother was initially frightened by the bandages which wrapped the face of her young son after he was released to her. She was reassured that, once the bandages were removed, he would be the handsomest boy in all the town. Her joy was overwhelming. Other operations were orthopedic in nature, like that of a youngster who underwent a double-club-foot procedure. It would allow him to walk normally and to wear shoes for the first time. He left the hospital with a huge entourage of happy relatives surrounding him.

One evening, a dinner in a nearby town was held in our honor. Tables were set up in the back yard of a modest home. Music was provided by dubious but enthusiastic musicians; food was prepared by neighbors and folks came from all over the village to join in the festivities. We had such mutual feelings of friendship and unity! The highlight of the night was watching a young woman dance.

This pretty girl, years earlier, had herself been helped by some of the same American medical people who were now watching her perform. Back then she had been frail. And now she was dancing!

When Lora and her grandmother finally made it to the clinic it was obvious that the child was gravely ill. She was examined almost immediately. Tests proved that she had critical heart problems, and, without help, would probably die within a month. Quickly, phone calls were placed to the United States to find a heart surgeon and hospital who could accept her on such short notice. Arrangements were then made for her visa and passport, while a foster family was lined up, and her airline reservations were made. By the time the team was ready to return to America, miraculously, Lora was able to go too.

Months later I flew to Nicaragua again, this time simply as an escort for two returning children. One of them was Lora. How can I possibly describe the difference between the energetic, playful and healthy girl of the present and that sick, listless and barely-breathing child of the past? Can you imagine the reaction of her *abuela* who once again had traveled for hours to meet us? She picked that little girl up in her arms and smothered her with kisses and hugged and hugged her. Then I watched this stoical woman's eyes slowly brim over with tears of joy and relief.

I have other poignant memories of this medical mission which will always be etched in my mind. In my heart, I wanted to instantly become a doctor myself and somehow cure all of the sick or injured children I met. But this story is not about what I saw, or what I didn't do. It's about a marvelous yet unassuming group of people: doctors, nurses, mothers and fathers, Nicaraguans and Americans. All were joined together under a common humanitarian goal. In a faraway country, they SAW – and DID!

CLINIC

On all HTC-organized medical missions, prospective cases, whether needing surgery or not, are initially seen in a chaotic environment called "Clinic." This examination setting consists of at least one doctor (the pediatrician and often the surgical doctor too) a nurse, translator, photographer and a few local assistants who try to maintain the order of children and parents coming in and out. Almost all the kids are brought by their mothers. For the smallest ones, the experience can be terrifying, accompanied by shrieks of fear and pain. In Nicaragua, the clinic rooms are rarely air conditioned, and the curtains dividing the examination area is torn and dirty. Nevertheless, this is where some big decisions are made. Will this ailing child need surgery or just be treated with medicines or therapies? Will this toddler need to go to the United States for a critical medical procedure that can't be performed locally? Will a sobbing mother be told that her child just can't be helped at all? (I've witnessed a doctor gently conveying this terrible news. Then I watched him leave the room to quietly weep.) On the other hand, when a sobbing mother is told that, yes, her child CAN be helped, this announcement creates faces lit up with absolute joy.

One day in clinic a man came in. He'd ridden there on a motorcycle along with his son. The father still had his helmet on and looked to be the epitome of a young, macho, Latino dad. In his interview with the doctor, he said that his son had been *eating dirt* and he wondered why.

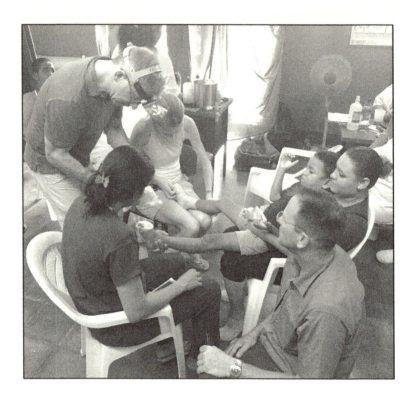

It turned out that the boy was malnourished. If more fruits and vegetables were added to his diet, he would quickly stop eating dirt, become healthier and remain that way. What a simple remedy! The father assured us that he'd follow through on this.

At that moment, though, this macho young father turned slowly to all of us who were in the clinic at the time. It quickly became apparent that he had originally thought there was something *horribly* wrong with his son. The fact that the cure was only a matter of a diet change was a complete surprise. In fact, it was such a profound relief that he was almost speechless. Tears formed in his eyes and slowly trickled down his cheeks while he clutched his son to his chest. Then, haltingly, he said, "I…..I…..I do not have the words….I do not know how to thank you…"

But then, pointing upwards with his finger, he said, "But HE knows." Making the sign of the cross, he smiled at all of us and left the room. We cried too.

FOUR

During a medical mission to Central America, a nurse from the Nicaraguan hospital where we worked, came somewhat tentatively into Clinic and asked if she could see the doctor. She was about twenty – older than the kids we usually accepted. However, there was no one else waiting so we made an exception. Our pediatrician then took her behind closed curtains.

After ten or 15 minutes the nurse stepped out of the examination area, smiled at all of us, left Clinic and went back to her nursing duties at the hospital.

Stepping out from the curtain, the pediatrician had a very unusual look on his face. We asked what happened. What had he seen? Was she okay?

Our doctor replied, "I've heard folks talk about cases like hers, and I've seen pictures of similar cases too. I even remember reading about anomalies in med school. However, I've never seen anything like it myself!"

He kept us in suspense a little longer. Meanwhile, we kept wondering. What was wrong with her? Why did she want to be seen? With that, the doctor replied, "She has four breasts. Two on each side, perfectly formed and perfectly functional. Her mother also had four breasts, as did her grandmother. Unbelievable!"

The Nicaraguan nurse had wanted to find out how difficult the surgery would be to remove two of them. Would it hurt a lot? Would she miss work? Was it expensive? Armed with information and advice, she made no immediate decision but promised to think about it.

Of all the cases he'd ever encountered, this was one our pediatrician said he'd probably never forget. Nor will we! She never returned to tell us about the choice she had made.

85

THE ESCORT

The Salvadoran airport was a hot and crowded place,
And nowhere could I find even one familiar face.
My journey to this country
had been made with all due speed:
For I was to accompany a child in desperate need.

The youngster's name was Pedro and 'twas he and I alone,
Who'd leave his native land
and the loving home he'd known,
To a stranger's house so far away he couldn't understand,
To an unfamiliar culture in an almost-magic land.

His parents saw me instantly; their eyes just seemed so sad,
As they steeled themselves to give to me
the only child they had.
I processed both the tickets and checked our baggage too.
It seemed to be one hectic blur,
when we were finally through.

Then the dreaded moment came
for his folks to say goodbye,
And as they placed him in my arms, they both began to cry.
Pedro, too, expressed his fears by sobbing mournfully,
And joining with them all were
the tears that came from me.

I carried little Pedro to our seats out on the plane,
While thinking of his parents,
who had been in so much pain.
"Let our son be healed" –
this they both did trust and pray.
Yet they couldn't hide their anguish
 as they saw us walk away.

In another crowded airport, other folks began to wait:
A nervous hosting family, together at the gate.
The mother held a teddy bear, the father a balloon,
Waiting for a frightened boy and hoping it was soon!

After seven tiring hours we landed at O'Hare,
And then I gave him over to the family waiting there.
I placed the sleepy Pedro into his a stranger's arms
But smiled at how trustingly he gave in to her charms.

The next few months passed quickly
for most everyone involved.
Pedro's desperate problems were,
through surgery, all solved.
And soon his wondrous doctors
found him absolutely healed,
And so, to me, "Please bring him back,"
his family appealed.

Then the dreaded moment came for his folks to say bye.
As they placed him in my arms, they both began to cry.
And Pedro, too, expressed himself by sobbing mournfully,
And joining with them all
were the tears that came from me.

This time, our airplane ride was happy and sublime,
And healthy Pedro laughed and played
throughout our flying time.
I had taken from his country a sick child, full of fright,
I now returned him gladly to a future that was bright.

In the window of the airport, I saw his mom and dad.
They pointed, and they shouted – they were so very glad!
Their tears of sorrow now were changed to those of joy:
I, the lucky escort, brought them home their precious boy.

BEACH BREECH

At one of Healing the Children's medical missions to Nicaragua, we were joined by a new pediatrician, Dr.
Jeffrey Karasik. He was a great guy, kind and gentle. He also had a few, quaint, East-Coast colloquialisms which I enjoyed hearing, such as his insistence that gym shoes were called "sneakers". At any rate, the team that he and I were part of, plus the other doctors and nurses, opted to spend a few hours on the beach one afternoon. Surgeries had ended early. All we had yet to do on the mission, visiting our previous surgical cases, was taking place the next day.

The beach was beautiful, and the water refreshing. Some of the team wanted to walk around for a while, many others wanted to wade and swim in the water. I opted to stay behind and keep an eye on everyone's personal belongings as they went off in various directions.

While they were gone, I was approached by a local resident who was carrying a big plywood sheet upon which had been attached dozens and dozens of sunglasses. He put the display down in front of me and asked if I wanted to buy any. I declined. However, a half hour later the same guy was back in front of me, carrying the same display! Once again, he asked if I'd like to buy any sunglasses, and once again I said no.

A few minutes later, the folks who had been in the water came back. Among them was Dr. Karasik. Suddenly I heard him callout, "Hey!" he said, "Where are my sneakers?!"

Our search was fruitless, and I concluded that after the sunglass salesman had placed that large display sheet down in front of me, he'd secretly grabbed a nearby pair of gym shoes. They were Dr. Karasik's!

Poor Dr. Karasik, now barefoot, was able to walk to a nearby beach shop where he purchased some colorful flip-flops. The thought of him wearing them the next day in the hospital and on the flight home too, was not a happy one. Fortunately, when we got back into town, we located a store where he could buy some clogs to wear – not the same as the nice shoes he had on the beach, but better than flip-flops. Ever since that trip, I'm confident that Dr. Karasik will always think of it as the one where the sneaky thief sneaked his sneakers.

FOREVER CHANGED

The pictures on this page show the wonderful impact our doctors can have on Healing the Children cases. I just love sharing these before-and-after photos.

Plastic Surgery Cases: The four examples below were done in Nicaragua and Ecuador:

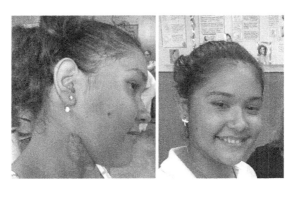

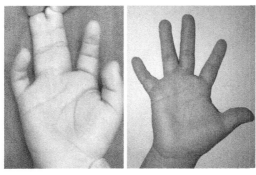

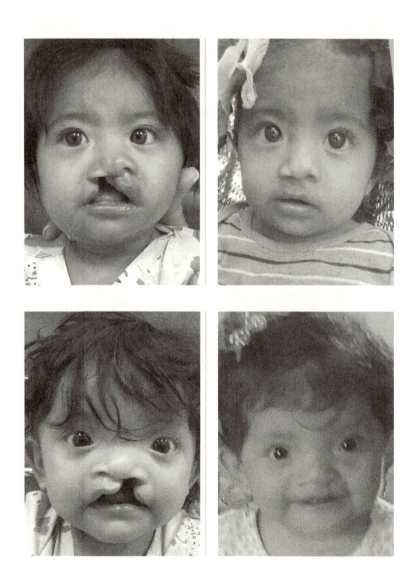

Cardiac Electrophysiology Cases: These two examples involved the repair of severe tachycardia and were both done in Illinois

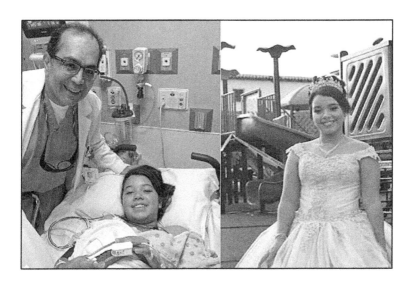

93

FROM NEEDY TO NEEDED

Here are two heartwarming examples of kids who were once sick or disabled – and now have become physicians themselves. Both were motivated to do so by their own experiences as Healing the Children cases.

ASHANTI – Saying goodbye to her foster dad after otolaryngological surgery. Now she's **Doctor** Ashanti, practicing in Florida.

HENRY – With his parents in Nicaragua before flying to the United States for heart surgery. Now he's Doctor Henry, a pediatrician in Peru.

IZABELLA AND MARIA

I first became involved as a volunteer with Healing the Children because of a friend and fellow Delta employee, Vikki Bearman. She was a flight attendant who lived in Milwaukee, and she was familiar with the Wisconsin chapter of HTC. Vikki also knew that I spoke Spanish. One day she asked me if I'd be interested in flying to Guatemala to escort a 14-year-old girl, Izabella, back to Chicago. There her foster family would drive her the rest of the way to Wisconsin. It sounded interesting, and I readily agreed. Within a few weeks, I was on my way to meet Izabella and her family. She had been born with a small, dangerous hole in her heart. This condition could be cured forever by the cardiac surgery she'd undergo in the United States. I was able to spend one night in her home, meeting her mom and nine brothers and sisters. What an experience! Her older brother took me on a half-day tour of the area, including visiting the ruins of Antigua, the former capitol which had been destroyed in an earthquake. He also slept on the couch so that I could have his bed. I noticed that in the bathroom there were only two well-used toothbrushes. There were 10 people who shared them. At dinnertime, I noticed that nobody was eating. Finally, Izabella said to me, "We're waiting for YOU to start!" They also asked me what I usually had for breakfast. I said, truthfully, "cereal." Thus, on the breakfast

table that next morning was a brand-new
Chockulas!" The graciousness of her entire
wonderful. I would notice this same trait repeate
Central American family I met.

Eventually we left Guatemala City for Chicago and for the
entire flight, Izabella could hardly contain her excitement. Her
surgery was a complete success and soon afterwards she was
back home in Guatemala.

Some ten years later, I made another HTC escort trip to
that same country. Meeting me at the airport was beautiful,
healthy, 24-year-old Izabella. She drove me to a nearby
restaurant as we happily reconnected. Izabella and I are still in
touch with each other. She is now a multi-lingual U.S. citizen,
living in Washington DC, married to a wonderful man and
enjoying motherhood.

One year after my experience with Izabella, Vikki
Bearman and I had the chance to fly together to pick up a
terribly ill baby, named Maria, in Nicaragua. In fact, this baby
probably would have died had Healing the Children not
stepped in. Suffering from serious heart and lung issues, she
was extremely fragile, weak and quite underweight. Her tiny
body was so sick she didn't even have the strength to cry. I'll
never forget the look in her weeping mother's eyes as we took
Maria from her at the airport in Managua. Hope? Fear?
Anxiety? She'd possibly never see her child alive again. What
faith she had!

Here are photos of Maria that were taken on our flight to
Chicago from Nicaragua

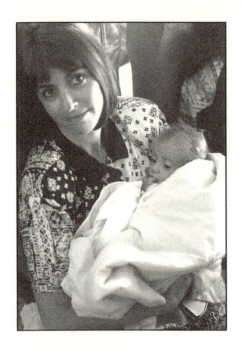

Maria's surgery was long and complicated and at one point she went into full cardiac arrest. Vikki Bearman had shared Maria's hospital stay with many people. Thus, every day this sick little baby had visitors! Most simply reached out to her tiny body and gently touched it, <u>willing</u> her to get better. Construction workers were building an addition to the hospital at the time. Many of them came in to visit Maria, some with tears in their eyes. They read to her, sang to her and prayed aloud for her. In addition, there was a guest book in her hospital room. Every person was invited to write something in it, and it ended up being full of the most wonderful, loving, supportive comments – all for a helpless child who was a total stranger.

Maria in the Hospital, intubated

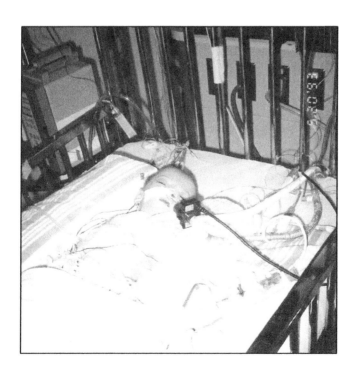

Maria eventually was released from the hospital and began an incredibly fast recovery, eating and eating, getting bigger and stronger, as if she was making up for lost time.

Here she is, just a couple of months after her surgery.

Six months after her arrival in the United States, Maria was ready to go back to Nicaragua. Vikki, now pregnant with twins, was unable to make the trip with me. So, I brought little Maria back myself, and the reunion of her with her mom was incredibly poignant. I smile every time I think about it. After that, Maria and her mom were waiting for me at the airport in Managua with every trip I made, whether as an escort or as a medical team member,. As the years went by, Maria had her name changed, and she is now called Vikki, after Vikki

Bearman, who first carried her in the journey that saved her life. I'm her "Uncle Jeff." Finally, here's a more recent picture of her, in the same pose as when she was a fragile baby, so many years earlier. She is now a healthy, happy, vibrant adult, and she and her mom have shared their own story with *future* scared mothers and children in the Nicaraguan airport, full of anxiety about saying goodbye to their own precious child.

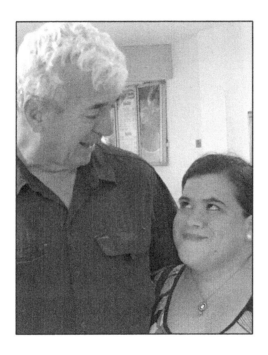

Daisy

Meet Daisis. She is the youngest daughter of a poor family in Nicaragua and appeared in her mother's arms during one of our medical missions there. I told her mom that, here in the United States, we could take care of the abnormal growth on her upper lip and that, upon her return, she'd be so pretty! Her mom wept and gave us the permission to enable her daughter to come to Chicago for plastic surgery. During her stay here, we all called her "Daisy." Then, after a team of Illinois plastic surgeons removed her large, upper lip tumor, Daisy became just as lovely as the flower we named her after. She's now nine years old: thriving, healthy, and an energetic schoolgirl.

Ingrid

I first met Ingrid in 1994, as her Healing the Children escort from Managua, Nicaragua to Chicago. She was tiny, frail, weak, and born without an esophagus. Weeks later, in a Milwaukee hospital, a complicated surgery created a new esophagus for her out of a section of her lower bowel. During that surgery, her heart stopped twice. Her ultimate recovery was long and difficult, as Ingrid learned how to eat and swallow solid food. The first picture shows Ingrid and me, coming to Chicago in 1994

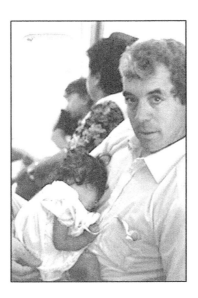

Ingrid and I did not see each other again for almost 20 years. During that time, she had returned once more to the USA for further medical treatments. Eventually, she was adopted by a loving family in Wisconsin because she would never be able to thrive in her native country.

In Milwaukee, she grew up much like other children and eventually chose to get her higher education at St. Norbert College, coincidentally, my own alma mater! In December of 2013, we met in the student union on the college campus. This was the first time I had been with Ingrid since carrying her in my arms as a terribly sick baby so many years earlier. When I saw her again, I cried.

Today, Ingrid remains healthy and happy. She is now the Executive Assistant and marketing team member of a performing arts center in Eau Claire, Wisconsin. She also assists with the management and design of an ice cream shop owned by her fiancé, Jeremy. We still keep in touch with each other. Her life is certainly different here, as she has easy access to quality health care, educational advancements and all the wonderful benefits of a U.S. citizen that the rest of us sometimes take for granted.

ENCIRCLED

I once flew to Nicaragua with a plastic surgeon, Dr. Nick Retson, as a scouting trip for a future medical mission we were planning there. Our return home was via Atlanta. Coincidentally, a little girl needed to be escorted there for the Florida/Georgia Healing the Children chapter. She was facing delicate eye surgery and we were glad to be able to do this.

Prior to leaving for the airport, Nick and I had breakfast in our hotel restaurant. There we struck up a conversation with a friendly lady, "Marcia" who was the leader of a church group. These folks were on our same flight to Atlanta, after spending two weeks in Nicaragua helping build a chapel and doing missionary work.

At the airport in Managua, we met tiny Katrina for the first time. She was about two years old, had a big patch over one eye, and was crying softly. When her mom gave her over to me, her gentle sobs turned into outright screams! Dr. Retson and I were both flying standby on Delta but were fortunate enough to get seats assigned in first-class. Being a doctor, I thought he'd be the perfect person to take the screaming toddler on board and he happily did so. But this made no difference to Katrina who continued to wail and cry, louder and louder. At this point, Nick gave Katrina to me. Uh oh! As other passengers in the first-class cabin started to look annoyed, I did my best to try and comfort the screaming little girl. The flight backed out of the gate, we taxied, took off and were soon flying above the clouds, which I pointed out to Katrina. It made no difference. I never knew a little child could cry so hard or so long!

At that point, I felt a tap on my shoulder. Marcia had made her way into our cabin from her seat in coach. Looking down at the crying girl – and perhaps my helpless eyes – she said, "Do you think I could take Katrina for a while?"

I'd like to say that I manfully hesitated. But that toddler-transfer from my arms and into hers broke all records. In the next instant, Marcia turned around, murmuring quiet Spanish to Katrina, (it did no good) and went back to her seat. Whew! Nick and I were both relieved, as were, I'm sure, the other passengers in First-Class.

I lost track of time for a while, but then, perhaps some thirty minutes later, I realized that there was no crying sound coming from the coach cabin. Huh? I had to investigate! What had Marcia done to soothe little Katrina?

I will never forget what I saw. Marcia was holding a sleeping Katrina on her lap. Her hand was gently placed on Katrina's head. But her *other* hand was holding the hand of another missionary. And that missionary was holding another hand. In fact, there was a literal **circle** of the people in her church group, all who had come from their respective seats. Other passengers had changed their own seats, enabling the entire church group, standing behind and to the side of Marcia, to form a hand-holding circle. These lovingly joined hands completely enclosed the area of the contented child, looping its way back to Marcia. All of them were praying silently. Katrina slept all the way to Atlanta and was still asleep when I watched her peacefully accepted into the arms of her host mom. Amen!

OW!

One of my HTC trips to Nicaragua was to pick up a three-year-old boy. He was the only case that I'd be bringing back. On the morning of our flights back to Chicago, I met his parents at the airport and found out that his preferred name was "Tomas." Our goodbye scene was peaceful, and Tomas and I quickly passed through the various Nicaraguan check points. We were on the plane in no time.

We had a four-hour layover in Houston. I was able to get one of the airport's luggage carts and put Tomas in the child's seat. He loved it! As time went on, a bathroom stop was necessary. Taking him down from the cart, we both went in and did our business, concluding with washing our hands. This is where things got difficult. The flow of water for the bathroom sink was triggered by a floor-level bar that simply needed to be stepped on. No problem! However, as I stepped on the bar and washed my hands, I noticed that Tomas was too little to reach the water. Keeping the water flowing, I eventually picked him up in my arms and stretched his little hands out into the stream.

Unfortunately, as I'd kept stepping on the bar, the water had gotten hotter and hotter. I certainly didn't know this would happen. That is, until I stretched his little, trusting hands into the now VERY HOT water. Tomas gave out a bloodcurdling scream, jerking his hands backwards and looking at me balefully, wailing at the top of his lungs.

I felt terrible! It seemed like it took forever for him to calm down while I soothed his hands. Fortunately, no harm had been done. Eventually, he was happily back in the cart.

An hour or so later, I passed a drinking fountain and stopped to get a sip of water. Tomas wanted one too. But sitting in the cart, he couldn't quite stretch far enough to reach the faucet. I got the cart closer…still no luck, though he tried valiantly. Finally, I <u>lifted </u>the front of the cart right off the ground and positioned it directly next to the fountain. Unfortunately, his little hand had been clutching the right side of the cart. And now it became painfully JAMMED against the side of the fountain! Oh my God! The screams and wails this time were even louder than those in the bathroom! Other passengers in the terminal even stared at me, as if I was brutalizing the poor boy. Over and over, I told him, "*Lo siento!* *Lo siento!*" (I'm sorry! I'm sorry!") He finally calmed down, had some rewarding gulps of water from the evil drinking fountain and off we went again.

I am happy to say that the rest of our journey to Chicago passed without further incidents. His surgery was a success, and a couple of months later Tomas returned to Nicaragua, though this time with a different escort. Do you think he missed me?

ROADBLOCK

Of the dozens of trips I've made for Healing the Children, all of them have been to Central America, primarily Nicaragua. This is a terribly poor country with a long history of political unrest, poverty, and oppression. Yet, except for a few isolated occasions, I've never felt uneasy or sensed danger in any of the journeys I've made there. One of those exceptions occurred when I was bringing a little boy back to Managua after his successful surgery in the United States. My flight was on Continental Airlines, and the routing took me from O'Hare to Houston, where Miguel (age 8) and I changed planes. Then we were to fly from Houston to Managua with an intermediate stop in Guatemala City.

An hour or so before arriving in Guatemala, the captain made an announcement, stating that a landing in Nicaragua might not be possible because of an ongoing "civil disturbance" in Managua. All Nicaragua-bound passengers were given the chance to deplane in Guatemala or to stay onboard, knowing that if the plane would not be allowed to land in Managua, it would have to continue to Honduras, the final stop of the flight.

This was worrisome, to say the least. I opted to stay on board and hoped for the best. When we landed in Guatemala, not one Managua-bound passengers got off.

As we got closer to Nicaragua, the captain again came on the air and told us, to our relief, that the plane would be allowed to land in Managua. There were cheers and claps of applause throughout the plane! However, he cautioned, all the roads leading to the airport were barricaded. No private cars, hotel shuttles or commercial vehicles of any kind could get to the airport. All shops and facilities inside were shut down.

Therefore, any arriving passenger faced the possibility of spending the night in a closed-down Managua airport. It was hoped that the civil disturbance would be over by morning.

The plane landed without incident, and Miguel and I easily passed through customs and immigration. In the Managua airport, there are huge glass panels separating the public area from the immigration area. Normally, these windows are jammed full of anxiously waiting family members. Not so this time. The only two people waiting there were Miguel's parents. What a wonderful surprise! They had heard rumors of the impending road closures and had left for the airport many hours earlier, taking smaller, side roads and avoiding the main highways. Good move!

As Miguel and his happy parents said goodbye to me and headed off to their car, I was left alone. They assured me that they had a "secret" way to get home. The airport had become deathly still, and the usual throng of taxis and cars in front of the arrivals area did not exist. Even the baggage porters and food vendors had disappeared.

My hotel was across the street from the airport, no more than a half-block away. But my late-night walk there was one of the most unusual I've ever taken.

The main highway which passes in front of the Managua airport is normally a very busy thoroughfare, encompassing six lanes of speeding, weaving cars and trucks. As an HTC volunteer, I've always stayed at this same hotel, a Best Western, which is clean and safe. But crossing that highway to get to the hotel has always been challenging. There are no traffic lights anywhere nearby. On this notable evening, however, this hectic boulevard was completely empty: no cars, no buses, no trucks, nothing.

In the distance, I could see a large pile of debris which had been set on fire, completely blocking all the lanes of traffic.

It was also eerily quiet, without the normal cacophony of airport and highway sounds...except for the occasional gunshot. Alone, I made my way across the dark and empty airport parking lot and over the deserted six-lane avenue. Soon, I found myself in front of the hotel. To the left and right of the doors were two young, Nicaraguan soldiers, each carrying an automatic rifle. It was at this moment that I felt the most out-of-place I've *ever* experienced in any foreign country. I wasn't scared, but I sure was uneasy

Inside the Best Western, the check-in desk had only one clerk. The hotel was without its main power supply and relied on generators to light up some of the main areas. I was led to my room by flashlight and all night long, the lights and air-conditioning continued to flicker on and off. Somehow, though, I fell deeply asleep.

The next morning, I stepped out the front door of the hotel, prior to walking back to the airport. Everything was completely back to normal! Once again, I could hear the familiar airport din, and I *almost* appreciated dodging those speeding, beeping cars, as they rushed along the boulevard again.

CHILDREN'S MIRACLE NETWORK HOSPITALS

Delta is a sponsor of a wonderful charity called "Children's Miracle Network Hospitals." This organization is self-described as "a nonprofit charity that raises funds for children's hospitals in the U.S. and Canada." Among other celebrities, Marie Osmond and John Schneider are quite involved. In 2006, because of my volunteer work with Healing the Children, I was chosen as Delta Air Lines' recipient of the "Children's Miracle Network Award." Marcie and I were flown to Orlando for a three-day weekend, during which I met some of the most amazing kids, all of whom had recovered from or been treated for terrible illnesses or accidents. The highlight of the weekend was held in a huge auditorium where six special honorees were invited to give short presentations about their work. I felt humbled to be one of them. Eventually, I found myself speaking from a stage in front of hundreds of attendees. Two teleprompters displayed, word-for-word, the presentation I'd prepared, and my image was simultaneously broadcast on a jumbo screen. It was so exciting! Next to me were Osmond and Schneider. If you'd like to see the speech I made, access YouTube on your computer and go to the search icon. Then just search for "Jeff Degner." Scroll down to "Miracle Awards" and you'll see a side of me passengers and employees at O'Hare *never* witnessed!

GREEN, BUT NOT
WITH ENVY

On one of my trips to Nicaragua, I was accompanied by Terri Klatt, a good friend and Delta flight attendant. We were to bring back three children in need of medical attention, one of whom was a toddler. The toddler, I felt, would be in good hands with Terri, who had raised two kids of her own. His name was Johan, and as it turned out, he had some serious gastro-intestinal problems and needed to be fed through a stoma (plastic, sterile tube) in his abdomen. His mother fed him before departure and assured us he'd be fine all the way to Chicago.

She was wrong. Halfway through our journey, Johan started crying and crying. Terri eventually concluded that he was hungry. Hmmm. Now we were faced with the challenge of giving him liquid nourishment, using a turkey-baster type of device, through the stoma in his stomach. We all had seats in the first row of coach.

Out of courtesy to the other passengers and to ensure privacy during this delicate procedure, Terri and I decided to both go with Johan into the airplane's First-Class lavatory. The flight attendants readily agreed. It was a tight fit with all three of us in that little bathroom!

We allowed Johan to stand upright in the sink, while we carefully took off his t-shirt and exposed the many bandages wrapped around the stoma. As we got closer and closer to it, the smell became more awful. The stoma itself was oozing, and the odor had now become a stench. Glancing away from Johan for a moment, and perhaps hearing me trying not to gag, Terri looked my way.

"Jeff", she said, "Why don't you let me finish up here? You can just go back to your seat now."

I've never heard such wonderful words! Terri finished the job and brought a contented Johan back to our seats. That was when she told me that my face was still a little green, though not as green as when I was in that tiny bathroom. She said she was more worried about me fainting, than dealing with Johan's stoma. Of course, she was completely wrong about that. I only left the bathroom to give her a little more room. Surely you believe that don't you?

TAKE A BITE
OUT OF THAT

It would be nice if every single trip made by a Healing the Children escort went smoothly. Most do. However, many of these international excursions have unexpected surprises, challenges, or complications. For example, escort Bruce once volunteered to fly to Nicaragua to pick up a little boy destined for internal surgery here in the U.S.A. On the morning of his return flight, he expected to meet the child and his family in the airport's main lobby, as he had on previous trips. No one showed up! The family had made a last-minute, fear-filled decision to cancel. What a shame!

I've witnessed little girls from Nicaragua dressed like princesses for their trip to America, wearing white, communion-type dresses and pretty, patent leather shoes. On more than one occasion, though, those shoes have belonged to a little sister, or were long outgrown. Noticing a child's limping or painful steps, I have practically <u>pried</u> shoes off that were two or three sizes too small. In another instance, a little boy's blue jeans had to be changed. The belt that cinched them around his waist was so incredibly tight, I don't know how he even breathed. One older girl was a great help to the escorts who were traveling with her and several other children, all with medical needs. She kept her own nauseous feelings to herself until the plane's layover in Houston, whereupon she promptly threw up. That same girl, by the way, is now a successful American architect living in Florida.

One other time, a teenage girl, Fatima, from El Salvador, collapsed in the jetway as she exited the aircraft. The Houston airport paramedics were called and were on the spot within minutes. The stressed-out escort was quite concerned. It turned out that Fatima was dehydrated and exhausted from a sleepless night. She was given permission to continue to Chicago. Whew! Sometimes, too, the surprises came as a result of a communication breakdown between HTC here in America and the HTC office in a third-world country.

For example, Tegucigalpa, the capital city of Honduras, was once my destination for HTC, journeying there to pick up a four-year-old boy named Edwardo. He was born with a club foot but orthopedic surgery in Wisconsin would make him good as new. When I arrived, I was immediately met by the Healing the Children representative in that city. As we spoke about Edwardo, she casually mentioned, "Jeff, you know that he doesn't hear, don't you?" I didn't know this at all. Then she added, "He doesn't speak either." Another surprise! Suddenly, what had promised to be an easier escorting trip now had a couple of real challenges added to it. However, the HTC contact wasn't quite done yet. "He also can't eat solid food." Despite my complete shock, I smiled and said, "No problem."

The next day, Edwardo and I departed for Chicago. He was quite still as I took him away from his weeping parents, and we easily walked onto the plane together. Edwardo took the window seat. Then, however, I saw him press his face tight against that airplane window. His little hands reached out in the direction of his *madre* and *padre* who were standing in the gatehouse. Unable to speak, he made the most pathetic "nnn nnn nnn" sounds, as tears slowly coursed down his cheeks.

After takeoff, Edwardo seemed so alert that I wondered just how bad his hearing loss might be. I already knew that he was speech impaired. So, I tested his audio ability by loudly snapping my fingers right next to his ear. Nothing. I called his name out sharply, startling the passengers seated behind us. Nothing. Now I knew that he was truly unable to speak or hear.

An hour or so later, meal service began on the plane. The flight attendant placed a tempting tray in front of me. It included a nice, warm bun, some potatoes and meat, and even a candy bar for dessert. Yummy! I told her that Edwardo would only be taking a beverage, rather than the normal dinner. He got a whole can of orange juice. I began eating my own meal but felt a little guilty. I felt even more guilty when I noticed Edwardo watching my every move, especially as I was placing food in my mouth. So, I decided to test, very carefully, what would happen if he had a morsel of my dinner roll.

I broke off a piece about the size of a pea and gave it to him. He popped it in his mouth instantly – and smiled! There was no adverse reaction at all, so I repeated this, very slowly and carefully, bit by bit, until the entire roll was gone. He was delighted.

Eventually, I added a few small bites of mashed potatoes, but stopped short at giving him any meat, nor any part of the candy bar that appeared very attractive to him.

The rest of our trip to Chicago passed uneventfully, and I told his host family everything that had happened. A few days later, I got a call from them. His surgery was over and had been very successful. Though they confirmed that he was hearing-impaired, the fact that he could make any sounds at all was a good sign. There was even a chance that, with special-needs training in Honduras, he'd be able to speak. Finally, they told me that there was nothing wrong with him eating solid food at all! We had no idea why Edwardo's poor parents had come to this conclusion, nor for how long his diet had been restricted. With this in mind, though, his care-giving American family said that they'd never seen a kid enjoy eating so much. Who could blame him?

ODE TO A HOST FAMILY

The pensive girl said goodbye,
Her flight would soon depart
To her mom and dad and siblings,
from whom she'd be apart.
She'd be so far away from
the country where they dwelt.
Anxiety and sadness were just
part of what she felt,
While you waited for her presence
into your home and heart.

The health care that she needed
was a problem somewhat large,
Doctors in America said they'd
help, and there'd be no charge.
In her native land, she would
never get this care,
Her medical condition could
not be treated there.
So, to host this needy child,
your own family would enlarge.

You met her at the airport,
she had flown so many miles,
And hand-in-hand walked with her

through the crowded aisles.
And off you went together,
by car, straight to your house.
Where she was greeted warmly
by your enthusiastic spouse,
Who welcomed her with a hug
and lots of beaming smiles.

The hospital asked if you
 could bring her for some tests,
You watched the nurse put
probes upon her legs and chest.
And when the tests had ended
with a date of surgery near,
You calmly reassured her that
there was no need to fear.
Yet as that day got closer,
how could *you* not feel stressed?

The medical procedure
was complex and very long,
And you could only hope that
nothing would go wrong.
And when the doctor came to say
that all was good and great,
This joyous news, so wonderful,
was truly worth the wait:
This precious child, once needy,

would soon be well and strong.
Just a short time later,
she was waiting to depart
And leave behind your family,
of which she'd been a part.
To journey far away
 to the land in which she'd dwell,
It now was you who felt so sad,
 while bidding her farewell.
Yet this girl, forever,
would remain inside your heart.

SURPRISE! SURPRISE!

I flew with my dear friend, Andi, on an escort trip to Nicaragua. We had five kids to take back. Three were older teenagers. One was only two years old, and her name was Fanny Rosa Gone Sanchez (Nicaraguans have four names: first given name, second given name, father's surname and mother's surname.) We just called her Fanny. The final child was a boy, age 11, whose name was Carlos Alfredo Gutierrez Sanchez. We simply called him Carlos.

The three older children were so excited to be flying! We all sat near each other, and Andi and I shared their joy of taking off and flying above the clouds. At this point, Fanny was on Andi's lap, though she had a seat of her own. I was in a middle seat with Carlos next to me by the window. I kept trying to get Carlos' attention. "Carlos? Carlos?" But he ignored me, even to the point where I thought he might be hearing impaired.

Then Andi noticed something and pointed it out to me. Carlos was quietly sobbing as he looked out the window! He was scared or perhaps already missing his parents.

"Jeff, look!" Andi said. "He's crying! Why don't you see if he'll sit on your lap? Maybe that will comfort him."

Though Carlos was a bit too old to be sitting on my lap, I thought I'd at least give it a try. Much to my surprise, he clambered into my open arms willingly and soon was nestled on my lap. Then, to my greater surprise, I realized that he had wet his pants! Within seconds, my lap was soaking wet, too. Oh, no!

Carlos had a change of clothes in his carry-on bag. I did not and ended up wearing the same odorous pants for the rest of our trip to Chicago. Phew!

Meanwhile, Carlos, now in a nice, clean pair of trousers, went back to his window seat while I took turns with Andi holding little Fanny. The rest of the flight passed without incident.

The very next day, however, we were advised by the host families of two unexpected situations. One: Carlos NEVER answered to his first name and only answered to his second, given name, "Alfredo." We never knew! Secondly, we found out that *Fanny had scabies*. SCABIES! This is a contagious skin infestation caused by tiny mites that burrow into your skin, leaving pimple-like rashes behind. It is intensely itchy. Andi and I – and our spouses – immediately had to get a special ointment from the drugstore and slather it thickly on our ENTIRE BODIES, leaving it there for 36 hours. We also had to carefully clean every surface we might have touched after arriving home from Nicaragua. All sheets, towels, blankets, our on-board clothing, even the chairs we sat on, had to be thoroughly cleaned and disinfected. Those 36 hours, as we stayed coated with a viscous chemical with an unpleasant odor, seemed to last forever. During that time, we found ourselves checking and double-checking every little itch, watching for those telltale rashes. Fortunately, we escaped unharmed. From that moment on, though, any potential child coming out of Nicaragua was pre-screened for this condition. Pre-screening had always been done to eliminate just about any other disease. Until our fateful flight, though, scabies had somehow been overlooked. Never again!

THREE'S A CHARM

In 2015, I flew to El Salvador to meet and escort three teenagers back to Chicago. All were suffering from severe tachycardia, with frightening attacks that caused their heart beats to skyrocket. Consequently, for years they had carefully avoided any activity or food that might bring about one of those attacks. They couldn't run, jump, dance or play sports with other young people. They couldn't eat chocolate, drink coffee or tea, and had to stay away from stressful situations – even scary movies.

They were so thrilled to be leaving El Salvador. None of them had ever left the country before, nor had any of them been on an airplane. Here's a photo of Edwin, Daniella and Maya as we flew above the clouds.

All of them were staying at the same large home in Illinois. Each had their own room and their own bathroom, too. What a big change from the conditions of their home in El Salvador!

Their medical procedures were called "electrophysiological ablations." Basically, they had been born with, or somehow developed, a small but damaged "spot" in their hearts which occasionally caused significant arrythmia. After non-evasive, but detailed surgical procedures, (lasting three to four hours) each of those three damaged hearts was totally repaired. Furthermore, after a couple of days of recuperation, they were told that they could now do *anything they wanted*. They could act like normal teenagers!

Not long after their time of rest and recuperation had ended, their host mom heard a strange thumping sound one morning. It was Edwin, Daniela and Maya running up and down the stairs. Why? Simply because they could! Later, during their three-week stay in Illinois, it snowed. There is no snow in El Salvador. I have a wonderful video of them looking up at the sky, catching snowflakes in their hands and mouths, scampering about, whooping for joy, throwing snowballs and making snowmen and snow angels. The looks of pure happiness upon their faces are something I'll never forget. Their laughter was infectious, and I often recall it when those first, heavy, flakes start falling here every winter.

Edwin, Daniela and Maya are now healthy, happy young adults living in El Salvador. They are also humbly grateful to Healing the Children and *everyone* involved in two vastly different countries, while being aware of just how fortunate they are. What great stories they will always have, especially regarding their first – and perhaps only – snowfall.

YUMMY COOKIES

As I was about to leave the emigration area (restricted to passengers only) of the airport in Nicaragua, taking Marco with me (a 7-year-old boy heading to Chicago for vital surgery), his mother came rushing up.

"Here", she said. "Please. I have made some cookies for you. Have them on your flight home if you or Marco get hungry." Into my hands she pressed a container with quite a few cookies inside. I put it into my carry-on bag and proceeded with the journey I was going to take with her son. Soon we were airborne and on our way to our brief layover in Houston. Turbulence was expected for most of the flight, so there was to be no meal service.

It seemed to take forever to get through U.S. Customs in Houston, to the point that we had to rush to catch our connecting flight to Chicago. We got to the gate just in time to board, but once again, we were soon airborne and ready for the last leg of the trip. That's when I realized how hungry I was! I also realized there was no meal service between Houston and Chicago and that made me even hungrier! All we had were little bottles of water.

Then I remembered the cookies. Ahhh! Taking the container out of my tote bag, I opened it up and took in their beautiful sight and sugary smell. I gave three of them to Marco who immediately gobbled them down like they were heaven-sent. Then, practically salivating, I grabbed one for myself, broke about half of it off, and popped it in my mouth. IN MY ENTIRE LIFE I'VE NEVER TASTED ANYTHING SO DISGUSTING!

It was all I could do to keep from vomiting on the spot, though I did reach for the barf-bag from the seat pocket in front of me, just in case. I just can't describe how terrible this taste was, even after I drank the entire bottle of water to wash it down.

Marco seemed amused. I gave him two more which he again devoured with joy. Not me. I was forever done with them, though there were plenty left over.

When I finally walked into my own home, hours later, I swear I still had that vile taste in my mouth. I shared the story with my wife, after warning her not to even *touch* the ones still in their container. That is when I had a truly ingenious idea. We took the remaining Nicaraguan cookies and put them on a decorative plate, covering them with plastic wrap. Then I took them with me to work at Delta the next day. We always had early-morning briefings, so I left the house extra early to be one of the first to arrive at the airport. Carefully unwrapping the plate of cookies (they *looked* great!) I placed them in the center of our briefing table. Then I waited and noticed how that plate of treats was quickly dwindling. I was barely able to keep from laughing aloud as employee after employee approached the table, selected what seemed to be a tasty, sweet delicacy and then sat down, often exclaiming, "How nice! Someone brought homemade cookies!"

Then I watched all their happy faces instantly turn into horrid frowns. One after another, they leaped up from their seats and raced into the bathroom. Others used nearby wastebaskets. Not one person finished their cookie, no matter how small their first bite might have been. Then, slowly, everyone somehow realized that it was me that had brought them. I was lucky to escape unscathed. However, with subsequent trips to Nicaragua, more than one person begged me NOT to bring back any more cookies! This would not be the last time I would encounter these evil cookies. They were offered to the doctors and nurses in at least a couple of subsequent medical missions. They were also given to me again in the airport in Managua, with the thought that they'd go to a host family. Not! I figure it must be an acquired taste. You can be sure, though, that it's *not* a taste I'll ever acquire.

POCKET PANTRY

Have you ever read the materials in the seat-pocket in front of you on a commercial aircraft? Delta Air Lines flight attendant Nancy McMullen and I flew to Nicaragua together on one occasion, and those contents turned out to be quite significant. We would be returning with two children: an older girl named Patricia and a wee toddler named Dennis. Early on, we agreed that Nancy would be the toddler's primary caregiver. As we took off from Managua, Patricia acted like a little angel. However, Dennis began to cry, louder and louder. This went on for quite a while, and it seemed like Nancy could do nothing to help. Finally, I asked if I could hold the sobbing baby for a while. Voilà! Dennis seemed to settle calmly and comfortably into my strong arms. Nancy and I soon began chatting. After some thirty minutes, I turned to her and pointed out how quiet little Dennis had become, no doubt due to my manly charms and vast experience with babies. Nancy glanced my way, looked carefully at Dennis, and then with pure horror in her voice, shouted out, "Jeff! He's been eating the seat pocket card! Oh my God!" Sure enough, Nancy grabbed him off my lap and scooped from his mouth a huge WAD of mashed-up cardboard from the Emergency Exit brochure, surely saving him from choking. I hadn't noticed a thing! Needless to say, he started crying again, but Nancy never gave me another. chance. Too bad – there was still part of that seat-pocket card ready for his second helping.

LANGUAGE PROFICIENCY

The high school Spanish that I learned in Señor Giamalva's classes, (see story #8, "Facing the Reds") served me well in my career with Delta and just as well as with many Healing the Children experiences. However, there still were some occasional tiny glitches in my attempts to sound like a native Latino.

For example, in school I learned that the word for "old" was "<u>viéjo</u>." This really came in handy one day when I was on a guided tour of a Central American village. The highlight of the tour was a stop at a palatial home which was built in the 1600's but had been lovingly restored, at great cost, by its current owner. I wanted to acknowledge the venerable age of this house, and so I told the proud owner, in Spanish, "This house is certainly very *VIEJO*"

He looked stunned.

The tour guide quickly intervened. It turns out that in that particular country, "*Viejo*" doesn't mean "old." Instead, it means, "run down" or "decrepit." Instead, I should have used the word "*antigua*." Egads! I had terribly insulted the owner. Fortunately, with the help of the guide, my error was explained, and all was well.

On another occasion, I once spent several months organizing a medical mission to Nicaragua. When at last the day came for our trip to begin, we were so happy and excited to be journeying to this country. We knew that dozens of children with medical needs would be waiting for us. In advance of the trip, I recalled from my Spanish classes that "happy" was "feliz" (like *feliz navidad*") and "excited" was translated as "*exitado*". Much of my correspondence with Nicaragua had been through a lady physician at the hospital where we'd be working. She actually met us at the front door.

"We're so feliz to be here!" I told her in Spanish. I'm so *excitado to* meet you!" In the next couple of days, I had similar conversations with many of the parents of the children we'd be treating. Sometimes their reactions seemed terse, but I assumed that they were just worried about their kids. THREE DAYS into the mission, a bi-lingual, Nicaraguan nurse took me aside and said, "Jeff, *exitado* in our country only refers to one particular type of excitement, and it's *completely sexual* in nature."

OMG! I had told the Nicaraguan lady doctor that I felt *exitado* about meeting her! With all the parents, I had been telling them that we all felt so *exitado* (aroused) to be with their children! It turns out that the word I should have used was "emocionada." What a humiliating error. STUPID GRINGO! Fortunately, I avoided saying that I felt "embarasada" because in Spanish that word means "pregnant" Whew!

WET TOWEL

Once there was a little girl in Nicaragua who needed to come to the United States for a life-changing surgical procedure. She was 8 years old, and her name was Cristina. As an escort volunteer for the Wisconsin chapter of HTC, I was happy to go and get her. Then, as the date for my departure got closer and closer, it turned out that there was a very slight chance a *second* 8-year-old would also be ready to fly with me. Her name was Tierna. However, in addition to Tierna's medical problem, HTC had reason to believe she was suffering abuse at home. Therefore, getting her out of Nicaragua had some extra urgency to it. Nevertheless, Tierna didn't even have her passport, nor her U.S. visa, so the odds of her being ready to leave with Cristina and I were negligible.

I flew to Managua, spent the night at a nearby hotel, then left early for the airport. I was to meet Cristina and her family for the first time in the airport lobby. There she was, all dressed up in a pretty, white dress with matching shoes, looking like a princess. In her hand she carried a small hand towel, and I wondered what it was for. Then I saw her dabbing her eyes with it. It was a crying towel! As Cristina and I got ready to check in at the Continental ticket counter, I heard someone call my name. Turning around, I saw a second little girl, also in a pretty dress, and I realized that it was Tierna. Her parents had arranged for her passport and visa in record time and now were going to be entrusting her to my care. I was so happy to see her! HTC had already made reservations for her as well, just in case this fortunate event had happened.

As he began checking us all in at the ticket counter, the agent closely examined my passport, as well as the passports and visas for the two girls.

He frowned when he was looking at Tierna's passport. "Where is her departure stamp?" he asked. "She can't go without a departure stamp."

This was a big shock to me! I asked to speak with a Continental supervisor. Sadly, the supervisor said the same thing: No stamp, no go. The supervisor said that it was a Nicaraguan security rule that Continental had no control over. So, feeling more and more worried, I asked to speak with an airport security officer. Once again, I was told that without this critical "*estampa de salida*". Tierna would have to stay behind.

Now I was desperate. So, I asked to talk to the <u>manager</u> of security at the airport. This, by the way, had been taking quite some time, and through it all, Cristina, Tierna, and their families had been following my every move, looking more and more worried. Eventually, standing directly in front of the Nicaraguan security manager, I showed him Tierna's paperwork. "She has no departure stamp," he said. "I can't let her go without one." At this point, out of any other reasonable option, I looked him in the eye, raised my voice and said, "LOOK. THIS IS ABOUT A LITTLE GIRL'S LIFE! Are you going to let a simple departure stamp stand in her way? A hospital is waiting for her in America!"

With that, the manager miraculously changed his mind and escorted all of us back to the ticket counter. Cristina and Tierna now realized they'd be leaving their families and both girls began sharing that same crying towel, passing it back and forth and weeping aloud. Meanwhile, more and more time passed by while I checked us all in, got our three boarding passes and headed towards the security area. Once again, I presented the officials with the now-approved paperwork, passports and visas. Then everyone's hand baggage had to be put through the X-ray machines. One of the girls had a small bottle of water in her bag. This was removed, and the bag was put through another time.

I don't know if I've ever felt so stressed out. Yet, this is exactly when I heard my name being paged, "Jeffrey Degner, please report to gate 11 immediately." I knew that our plane was about to board.

Gathering up the carry-on baggage, paperwork and grabbing the two girls' hands, we rushed up a flight of stairs, down the long concourse and, finally, to the gate. We got there barely in time to pre-board. My heart was pounding, my face a sheen of sweat, and I was almost out of breath as we walked down the jet bridge and onto the plane. We were assigned seats in the first row of coach: 10A, 10B and 10C. However, no sooner had I started putting our carry-on baggage away when a flight attendant came to us from the front of the plane. She had gotten advance word that I was a Delta Airlines employee, escorting Cristina and Tierna for medical reasons.

"We have no one sitting in first class on this flight," she said. "Why don't the three of you come up front?"

What an unexpected and special gift she had given us! Therefore, Cristina and Tierna soon found themselves in seats 3A and 3B. I was across the aisle from them in 3C

That, my friends, is when I lost any semblance of composure. All the stress of the past two hours simply evaporated, and I knew that at last we'd soon be on our way. I'm not ashamed to admit that I just put my head down and started quietly sobbing. The wonderful flight attendant looked shocked and didn't quite know what to do, but Cristina and Tierna sure did. They promptly shared their crying towel with me! Thus, on that sodden towel there were tears of sorrow from two sweet girls saying goodbye to their families. There were also tears of pure relief from one grateful man, named Jeff.

Thank you for reading these memoirs. I'm forever grateful to my family, friends and colleagues for their support and encouragement over the years, and to the passengers, all of them unique, who made this second book possible. I also remain grateful to Healing the Children for giving me the chance to be a part of so many little lives. Many of them will live in my heart forever! As this manuscript was being created, I need to thank my editing guru, Fotena Zirps, as well as the many other folks who gave me their thoughtful suggestions. In addition, kudos go to Wasteland Press for putting everything together so nicely.

Lastly, I wish you all joy, love, adventure and health. Here's to the many runways you are yet to land upon!

ABOUT THE AUTHOR

Jeff Degner is a free-lance writer whose stories and poems have appeared in a variety of books, papers and magazines. With their senior canine, Luna, Jeff and his wife, Marcie, live in Barrington, Illinois. Both love to travel and during the winter enjoy cheering on their favorite NFL team, though it isn't the same one. Besides writing and dabbling in genealogy, Mr. Degner is an avid pickleball player. He also is the president of the Illinois/Indiana chapter of Healing the Children. In fact, proceeds from the sale of this book, as well as from "What Track for the Atlanta Flight" will be going directly to HTC. More information on Healing the Children can be found at www.healingthechildren.org or www.htc-il.org

Jeff is always waiting to see just whatever life's next adventure is, around the corner or around the world. Email him at: deltawriter90@gmail.com

Here's a final smile to last a while: Can you decipher the image on the back cover?

Made in the USA
Monee, IL
29 October 2021